TALL TALES BY A SMALL DOG

Tall Tales by a Small Dog

OMAIR AHMAD

SPEAKING TIGER

SPEAKING TIGER BOOKS LLP
125-A, Ground Floor, Shahpur Jat
New Delhi—110049

First published by Speaking Tiger Books 2023

Versions of 'Does It Catch Mice' and 'The Dog Thrower of Chhote Qazipur' were first published in *Brooklyn Rail* and *Indian Quarterly*, respectively.

ISBN: 978-93-5447-521-4
eISBN: 978-93-5447-522-1

10 9 8 7 6 5 4 3 2 1

Typeset in Baskerville MT Std by SŪRYA, New Delhi
Printed at Chaman Enterprises, New Delhi

For Apa, Ateeq bhaijaan, Atika—

'Yeh jo humari mitti hai...'

CONTENTS

PROLOGUE

Never tell anybody you are a writer, especially a dog. Every dog is a storyteller, but dogs do not write—you know, the whole thing about opposable thumbs and all. And once they find out you are a writer, they will want to tell you their stories, ask you to put them down, and they have so many.

Did I say they are storytellers? Well, that is a polite word, the damned things are gossips and divas, all convinced they are the artists and oracles of the age because they can sniff better than you and I. And they hear all the dog whistles too, far better than even the foot soldiers of the strongman.

They will tell their stories to one and all, and if

you do not write them down, they will tell stories about *you*—complicated, twisty things, with grains of truth mixed up with the spice of scandal, fantasy and heady lies, all wrapped around and slathered over the meat of the matter. Such a meal they will prepare for you, that you won't be able to tell if the bones are those of beast or man, or of which beast and what man.

The things they have howled about me across continents! It is so shameful, about women and boys, about forbidden drink and sinful meats, about silks and gold, blood and shit (and they love their gore!). None of it was true, of course, but presented with just the right touch of plausibility, barked loudly enough, and repeated across town and city in a chorus of agreement. Even I started wondering about myself! Before the power of their tales what could I do but flee, hide until the dark of the new moon, until people forget and move on?

Ah, but dogs don't. Forget and move on, that is. They are famous for it, for staying on a trail, for scenting the faintest whiff of a scandal—here and now, or in the moment yet to come—and chasing it, and leading all the world to the poor sod who would be most embarrassed by it.

We've all heard the story of how the dog accompanied Yudhishthira to the gates of swarga-lok itself, and that faced with Indra's unwillingness to allow them both into heaven, Yudhishthira was willing to exchange places with his loyal companion. We are told that the dog was Dharma himself, more faithful than brothers and wife. It is a great story, one of thousands in the greatest of all stories, told long before the firangi thought up their paeans to loyal hounds and terriers. Why, even the beloved Prophet Himself is said to have blessed a man who went down a well and brought up a shoe full of water for a thirsty dog, the very creature whose saliva is haram, for it eats anything and everything.

I gave in to the rascals, the sons of bitches who claim the nights with their howling and yammering, the FM radios of all the nights of Hindustan. This book in your hands is proof, if any was needed, of my cowardice and capitulation, of their long manipulation. But I had some little shred of dignity left. I set some terms, lines in the sand. Gorakhpur, I said, the land of my father, my father's father and his father's father before that—centuries of bones and flesh turning to soil and mud, nurturing the soil that has nurtured us, aeons of a snake eating its own tail—Gorakhpur, I said, must be the muse.

I knew the rascals would lie, spin fantastical tales, play with my mind and yours. And here, on my own soil, this soil mixed with the clay of my ancestors, I would stand some chance of fighting back, of taking the flights of fancy and tying them to earth, so that whatever tall tales I was fed, I could add a note or two of reality to them. I would defend the honour of my mitti, I thought to myself, the only honour they had not stripped from me.

In the end it was just one specimen of their biradari that they sent to me: Kallu, Kallu Maharaj, also known as kutta, kamina, harami, chor, and a string of more colourful names that my pen does not allow me to record. He seemed a nondescript character to have earned such fame from bakers and butchers, maids and washermen, a small dog of indeterminate colour and parentage, with a tendency to tuck in his tail and skitter away at the slightest sense of danger. But only to return, courting danger from a distance, until it was time to turn tail again. Wars have been won in such fashion, so for this, at least, I will not judge him.

A bit of a runt, then, this mongrel. Nothing remarkable about him.

It was only when you looked closely that you realised he had the oddest eyes—they'd glint disconcertingly, sometimes blue in the light of the sun, sometimes red in the light of the moon. It was the spookiest thing, and I politely broached the subject at Professor Malik's house at a quiet moment in one of his mehfils. He scoffed at the notion and told me to go easy on the liquor. I knew then that I had been forestalled, for it was only the dogs who told tales of my drinking. Somehow, they had planted their rumours even in the heart of the greatest zoologist of the region.

I did not enquire further, but I wondered about this dog, Kallu, whose tribe, we are told, cannot see colour, only black and white, with only their fantastic noses painting the world for them in vivid tones. How could I believe this about a dog whose eyes glinted in colour, and that too in different ones at night and in daylight?

And the tales he had to tell—delivered with the skill and poetry of a dastango, or mumbled from the corner of his mouth as he ate a samosa stolen from my plate, enjoying himself as I goggled at what he said. I have been told that Zen masters debate whether a dog has a Buddha nature, but who would have thought that a dog would be so informed about the Buddha's mother? And about tigers and shikaris and gangsters and banjaras and the wily firangis. About the Chinese who are now so Indian that they eat Gobi Manchurian and do not complain; about Gandhi and Kabir, and much else that I could never in any way confirm.

And they are all so mixed up, his stories, twisted, tangled and knotted, like the strings of the kites we used to bring down in our aerial battles back when we were boys. But I no longer have the wisdom of my youth, the felicity of mind and fingers, that I can untangle the knots and loops of any of Kallu's tales and tell where it begins and where it ends. In my tongue they say you can never straighten a dog's tail. How much more difficult to straighten a dog's *tales*, then!

Anyhow, I've set them down for you on these pages, Kallu's stories that are like our messy, twisty galis, like the complicated webs of cable and wire that hum and spark and sizzle above many a Gorakhpuri head. Only, be warned: these are the tales of a small dog, recorded. And all dogs are storytellers, and all storytellers are liars. Believe what you will of them, but believe at your own peril.

May the clay of my ancestors forgive me, and not turn me from my mitti.

THE DOG THROWER OF CHHOTE QAZIPUR

Allow me to begin with myself. A dog's own story, if you will. And let me begin at the tail end of it all.

That was the day that Bilal showed me the newspaper. The headline read: 'Soldiers Attacked by Wolf Monster'. Next to the story was a sketch of a huge hairy man-like thing.

'That's supposed to be us, Maharaj,' Bilal said, laughing his curiously soft laugh, more a snuffle than anything else—always a surprise coming from somebody as big as him.

I yelped along, but to tell you the truth I didn't

care about the story in the paper. I can't read, you know that, and the picture didn't make much of an impression either. All I was interested in were the pieces of choice meat that Bilal had wrapped in the paper. It was a rare privilege for me to enjoy such a meal, and that too from Bilal, the dog thrower of Chhote Qazipur.

Let me introduce myself now, so that you will see me, know something of me, in this first of all the stories I will have you write down; you will see me, and in me, all my brothers, sisters and cousins you may find in the stories that follow. All your stories are ours to tell, after all; we are everywhere, in your lives and your deaths, especially your deaths. And yet who knows us, who speaks our names?

They call me Kallu, Kallu Maharaj or Sale Harami, depending on whether I'm wagging my tail, doing a little trick or trying to steal a bit of meat from the butcher shop. I've been living in the galis of Chhote Qazipur ever since I was born here, raised for a few weeks by my mother and then abandoned, along with my other siblings, to fend for myself.

It was then that I started to explore my territory. Most people think that dogs are free to roam where they want. This is true, but only until one gets to the point where another dog has decided to roam. At this point things become interesting. If you're a small dog, like me, and all alone, you find your territory to be quite limited indeed. Many were the days and nights when I'd receive one hard smack on the snout and end up yelping and running back to my two-and-half alleys with my tail between my legs.

But I didn't give up. Maybe it was my personality that made me so adventurous, I was much too curious about the rest of the world. Or it was my nose. I'd smell food being cooked down the street and sneak up to take a look—only to find some mangy cur with his teeth bared, hair on end and a growl building up in his throat. And far bigger than me.

And it wasn't just the other dogs that I had to worry about. I remember my first taste of a hot samosa. It was spicy, sharp and so hot, it burnt my tongue for the half-second that I had it in my mouth. I had seen it sitting beside its brothers on a platter at the dhaba near the alleyway that passed for home. It was a big, fat samosa, and so lumpy that it was deformed. The dhabawala hadn't managed to sell it for the hour I'd been sitting watching, tongue out and drooling. This is a town of aesthetes, after all—I mean, *your* kind are, the fools; even a man with just two paise to his name might scorn a diamond the size of Gama's fist if it hasn't been cut to perfection. But the dhabawala was hopeful. He kept reheating the misshapen samosa and putting it at the edge of the platter. And he finally put it an inch too far. I had managed to sidle up almost to the entrance of the dhaba without arousing the man's suspicion, and now I leapt.

The platter overturned with a dreadful clash and clatter and the dhabawala hollered in anger, but I had that samosa in my mouth, its delicious fragrance rising up my snout as I landed back on my feet, prepared to speed off into my alley.

But it was not to be. I'd resisted biting down because of how hot the samosa was, and I lost a precious few seconds trying to readjust it in my mouth. It was long enough for the dhabawala to fling a heavy rubber slipper at me. It hit my ribs with a thump and I yelped, jumping in pain and surprise, and the samosa went spinning out of my mouth. Just for a second, I thought of catching it again, but the dhabawala was charging after me with his other slipper. Tail between my legs, mewling in fear, I fled for my life.

And the absolute worst bit of it was that just as I fled, I saw another dog nonchalantly pick up the samosa in his mouth and saunter off in the opposite direction. The hurt of that moment is still exquisite pain, like your first heartbreak.

It was also the time I was given a new nickname: 'Sala harami'. And the dhabawala used it every time he saw me after that.

You could say that samosa changed my life. Before that experience, humans had been faraway creatures. They existed, all right—I was always aware of them, never more than when they forgot to bathe—by god! sometimes the very stink of some residents of Gorakhpur is enough for me to think it should be called Gobarpur instead… Of course, some of them smelled good, putting on ittar before Friday prayers, and the bakers, cooks and butchers moved around in a cloud of the most gorgeous scents. But that was all the thought I gave them. Your kind were an irrelevance in my life until that samosa.

For days after I was deprived of it and thwacked with a half-kilo chappal, I glared at every specimen of the dhabawala's species. If I were a bolder dog, with the balls to be angry, I would have sunk my teeth into some ankles.

But then a really weird thing happened. I found a friend among your kind.

It didn't happen the way you might think it did. And to this day I sometimes want to run and hide when I see him. But he made me into something else, like how you say your ancestors trained and changed us from wolves to dogs, although it was probably we who taught you to stop being the monkeys you were.

This is how it happened. I had been trailing one particularly smelly specimen of the residents of Chhote Qazipur—you know the mohalla?—he had a samosa in his hand, he'd broken off a piece and was eating it as he walked leisurely along. A burly young man, he looked older than his age, and older than the friends who trailed along behind him. Seeing that samosa had brought out something in me, and I'd begun to follow him almost despite myself. I was trying to work up the courage to do something, when he looked down and saw me at his heels. '*Arre sale, tu kya kar raha hai*?' he growled, doing a much better job of being threatening than I ever could.

Caught between dreams of free food and suddenly finding myself confronted by a human, I froze.

'Let him be, Bilal,' one of the other humans said. 'Obviously the dog's in love.'

At this everyone started laughing, except Bilal, who glared at them. Unsure of where exactly this was going, I began to wag my tail slowly, uncertainly.

'*Dekho, dekho*!' one of the boys said, 'The dog is truly in love!'

I started to wag my tail faster.

As the other boys laughed, Bilal glowered at them, then at me and, after a moment, he too burst out laughing. '*Chalo*, at least somebody loves me, unlike you losers.'

Turning to me he broke off a bit of the samosa and threw it in my direction, '*Lo, Kallu ashiq*, have something to eat.'

I jumped, and snapped the morsel out of the air. It was heavenly!

I liked the name that came with the gift: Kallu.

'*Hai, hai*!' Bilal exclaimed, 'Kallu can dance.'

It was the beginning of a beautiful relationship. I became used to tagging along with Bilal and his gang, jumping about, playing the fool and, most importantly, being fed for my follies.

I'd been lucky. Bilal and his gang, largely consisting of Shakil, Munna, Asif and Amit—all of whom were interchangeable except for Bilal—owned the streets of Chhote Qazipur. Or the alleys, to be honest. Like many old towns in north India, Gorakhpur has old town areas that were built before the introduction of cars. The roads between houses were always narrow, and an ever-increasing population meant that old houses grew into the already narrow streets, creating a maze of galis that could only be negotiated on foot or bicycle…You say you know this? Well, well, isn't that a surprise, a Gorakhpuri who has the sense to actually see the streets he walks, instead of just using them to piss in the open gutter running beside them.

Write that down. Write it. This is my story, not yours, you are merely a hired scribe. Let *me* tell the world of your mitti and its people.

Yes, yes, efforts were made from time to time to expand the streets, cover them with tar, put in drainage, and most of them became just wide enough that your lot could drive a car through them, if you navigated very, very carefully. But the roads remained slim veins of civic authority winding through an old, scarred, twisted body bulging at the edges. Once in a while I'd come upon two cars stuck in some narrow passage that could barely accommodate one. They would be locked in an amusing contest of manoeuvring, moving an inch here and an inch there, farting clouds of black smoke, neither wanting to completely give way but the drivers too polite to fight.

In other parts of this town—all right, city, if you will—in other parts, they might have yelled at each other, rained down abuses, hurled insults implying that the other person's family would have had carnal relations with goats had the goats not spurned them. But not in Chhote Qazipur; this was a polite part of town, with old houses whose residents prided themselves on even older lineages. The neat, clean canal that led to the river, and thence to the sea, might have been built over, leaving only the name Reti—sandy—as a reminder of days long gone, but some of the past gentility remained. Even we dogs knew this. You could identify an outsider immediately, not just from his odd smell but also from his barking. Excessive yip-yapping was not encouraged in Chhote Qazipur.

So, when I tell you that Bilal and his gang walked the alleys late at night, that they were the known rowdies of the area, got into scrapes and fights, you have to understand the limits of their misdemeanours. They didn't carry weapons: knives, homemade pistols or bicycle chains. They didn't commit any crimes against the state; only against good taste. At most they would bully and push, swagger and strut.

This was Bilal's Gang, and I was a junior member.

But there is always a price to pay for membership. I had figured that my antics had earned me my place in the gang. But this was Bilal, and whereas he could be generous, he was also demanding. He'd hold up my front paws and make me dance, catch me by my tail and pull me along, flip me food that was too hot, and once even fed me a cube of ice hidden in a stale pakora. He confused me.

What I didn't understand then was that Bilal and his gang, much like their mohalla, were being hemmed in on all sides by growth, prosperity and modernity—what passes for modernity in our parts, anyway—but they had no access to any of this, certainly not Bilal. He didn't have the right education, or the right connections. The third child and only son of a postal employee who had died when he was, officially, not yet forty, unofficially forty-four-forty-five, Bilal had few chances in life beyond his work managing a warehouse.

It had been an excellent break for him at age seventeen. The warehouse was owned by an uncle of his, and Bilal's impressive physique and powerful personality kept most of the workers in line very easily. There was more to it than that—he was also demanding, as he was with me, and displayed a sense of ownership bordering almost on cruelty; if he could drag me after him by my tail to hurry me up, he could drag his workers back to the warehouse after midnight to unpack an entire consignment and spend fifteen hours straight packing it all over again because he did not like the shape of the cartons used. But with this came a sense of responsibility and a depth of care that was unusual. He cradled my body once, when I stepped on a shard of glass, removing it with care, and then bullied a doctor to clean and bandage the wound in double quick time. He did far more for his people, and they returned his care with hard work and loyalty. His uncle gave him a small raise after the first year, and then another one.

But five years into his job he was painfully aware that most of his childhood friends were passing him by. Occasionally a member of his gang too would dip his head in farewell, shake Bilal Bhai's hand, thank him for the good times and then ignore him on the street a few months later.

It says a lot for Bilal that he remained as generous as he was, but there was frustration there as well, a wish to show the world something. And then came that Rath Yatra, and the riots that followed in its wake. The end of the 1980s, but maybe the end of centuries, an entire age.

Yes, I know, we didn't have riots in Gorakhpur, certainly not in Chhote Qazipur. But we did have newspapers and rumours, remember? We heard about so many Muslims killed in a town a few hundred miles away, so many Hindus killed in some isolated village; about guns, curfews and bombs. A harried-looking couple returned from Bombay. Their small clothing shop had been looted after a riot and they swore that the same fabrics went on display at their neighbour's shop the very next day. I don't read, but I heard how the name of Urdu Bazaar disappeared from people's lips and Hindi Bazaar emerged, how Mian Bazaar transformed into Maya Bazaar. The loudspeakers in the mosques became louder and started to broadcast sermons as well as the call to prayers. The ringing of temple bells rose in pitch, and bhajans suddenly appeared on tape recorders. Dawn became hellish with the clatter of competing prayers. Some of us dogs decided to bark nonstop early one morning to drown out the noise but not even the ants of Gorakhpur noticed our protest.

In Chhote Qazipur, Amit stopped hanging out with the rest of our gang.

Nothing hurt Bilal more than this. Riots and deaths, arson and murder, even the creeping change of names and attitudes were all things that we heard about and put up with. None of these were things we had any control over, so we tried not to think about them. But friendship was something else. And Amit hadn't even said goodbye.

Amit had new friends, another gang. They sported saffron bandanas and walked with a new swagger, but they dropped off Amit at the borders of Chhote Qazipur, not entering our alleyways.

It was at the border that Bilal confronted them.

He hadn't meant to. It was just one of those things that happened. Bilal had locked up the warehouse after all the workers had left, and after checking that everything was as it should be, he retrieved a bottle of beer from the crate where it had been hidden away. This was a new ritual that had begun only a few months ago. But I'd learned that it paid to follow Bilal afterwards. He'd go to Qureishi's dhaba, and Qureishi would keep the place open just for Bilal, feeding him a plate of qorma and rice, sometimes biryani and kababs. They were rich pickings to be had. Once Bilal upended half a plate of lovely, lovely qorma on the street just for me, laughing as I went wild with delight, my tail waggling so furiously, making my entire backend shake, that I couldn't even eat properly.

This time though, we ran into Amit and his new gang on the way to the dhaba. All five of them.

'Oye Amit,' Bilal called out. 'I want to talk to you.'

Amit cringed. 'Bilal bhai…' he started to say, when one of the others, obviously their leader, stopped him.

'Don't call him bhai, he's no brother of yours.'

Bilal exploded. 'Behnchod!' he bellowed and lunged into the gang.

Had he been in his full senses he might have been able to handle them, but he was just drunk enough—and still unused to drunkenness—that his punches were off target and his footwork all over the place. They managed to surround him, and trip him. And once he was down, started to kick him.

I tried to do my best, but I hadn't been taught how to fight and was just barking like mad, spinning around them. Amit too was trying to do something, I don't know what, but he was equally ineffectual.

They'd underestimated Bilal, though. There was a lot of fire there, and after taking a few blows, he managed to get up on one knee. Blocking a punch with one hand, he grabbed an arm of one of his attackers with the other hand and pulled himself up.

There was a brief moment of silence, as Bilal faced the four men, panting and bruised, a full head taller than the tallest in that gang. He'd skinned his knuckles when he fell, and a little blood slowly made its way around his fist now and fell, drop by drop, on the road.

I went mad at that. Barking away like I had never done before as I stood between them.

'Quiet the dog,' the leader of Amit's new gang said, 'or we'll silence him like we silenced you.'

'Silenced me?' Bilal growled from behind me. 'Silenced *me*?!'

And then I felt his hands grab my rear legs. Before I knew what was happening, Bilal had lifted me up and was whirling me over his head. With a heave he threw me at his enemies. I slammed into Amit's new friends with a thump.

Completely out of my mind with fear and surprise, I bit and clawed, scouring faces and tearing shirts. Seconds later the streets were clear of everybody except Bilal and Amit, and yours truly, quivering with all my hair standing on end. Bilal was laughing uproariously. Even Amit was chuckling. Only I didn't get the joke.

After that evening Amit was back in the gang, but I started avoiding them. Every time I saw Bilal, or scented him, I'd be down the nearest alley and hiding under whatever I could find. Bilal would call after me, but I was too scared to present myself.

The funny thing was what happened in the rumour mills. Apparently, Amit's new gang, bitten and scratched, had ended up at the hospital. Unable to admit that they'd had a dog thrown at them, they cooked up a story about a terrifying wolf-monster and a sketch duly appeared in the local papers. Only in our neighbourhood did we know that the real terror was Bilal, the Dog Thrower of Chhote Qazipur.

This was all before the curfew days of the early '90s, as the riots edged ever closer to the city, after the mosque was torn down, just down the road, barely a hundred and fifty kilometres away in Ayodhya.

In the evenings I'd find people scurrying to do their final chores, and then suddenly the streets would be empty, with the occasional police patrol the only thing moving on the main roads. The racket of the priests and imams had also stilled and there was an odd peace despite the vague fear I saw on every human face—although I didn't see too many.

This was a great relief to my wounded confidence. Up till now I had never really appreciated just how much space humans took up, the noise and smells they generated. And now they were suddenly gone. No honking cars, no sputtering scooters or motorcycles, and no shrieking kids. For the first time in my life, I walked in the middle of the road and felt like a king. When I howled, a hundred dogs answered across the neighbourhood, well into other parts of the city. Suddenly, it was *our* city.

Or so we thought. We had not factored in the new hounds in fatigues.

After a few days curfew was relaxed. And then

imposed again—for longer hours and with a grim seriousness. Across the country the killings were picking up. The police were replaced by military units. Men were stopped and checked even during the day, and if somebody was caught after curfew, even a few minutes late, they'd be in trouble. Women found out that the police had a license to search them, leer at them, and stop them any time they pleased. One evening I saw a young man caught by a patrol. He told them he was coming from the railway station, even showed them his ticket, but they wouldn't listen. First, they made him empty his bags on the road, and after that they ordered him to take off his clothes. By the end of it he was standing naked, in only his underwear, while the soldiers mocked him, enjoying his fear and humiliation. They took their time letting him go.

Even the sudden freedom of us dogs appeared to be curtailed with the arrival of the hounds. I'd hear less barking. Sometimes the barking was cut off by mysterious yelps. Once, poking through the remains of a meal a patrol party had had earlier in the day, I came upon bones that were both familiar and strange.

One of the soldiers saw me and sneered, 'Don't like the taste? It was one of your brothers.'

The other soldiers laughed at that. It preyed on my mind all night. Was it a joke?

After that I kept a clear eye out for patrols, and didn't walk in the middle of the road. No more howling in the streets, either.

And skulking in the eerily quiet alleys, I ran into Bilal.

He had a scarf over his face, but his heavy, sweaty smell was immediately recognisable.

'Kallu Maharaj,' he said softly through the cloth. '*Kaise ho*?' Without waiting for an answer, he winked at me, and slid away into the gathering shadows.

I followed. This was a dog I knew, in alleys that were our own.

Quietly, Bilal crept along the alleyways, moving so silently yet swiftly that it was difficult for me to keep track. He stopped just before the alleys opened up to a chowk. A small army patrol was there, sitting by a fire, two of them drinking tea. Bilal took out a slingshot from his back pocket and a marble that glinted red and blue in the weird light of the streetlamps. Taking careful aim, he let fly.

With a sharp crack the marble split on a helmet and one of the soldiers was knocked sideways. The two tea drinkers spilled their drinks as they sprang to their jeeps and guns. By that time Bilal was long gone, sprinting along the alleyways with me running silently behind. Just near his house, he stopped. He was sweating heavily and panting like a bellows.

Undoing the scarf, he doubled over, hands on his knees. His breathing raw and ragged. I tried to lick his face, but he fended me away with a soft laugh. 'Ha, Kallu Maharaj, we showed them, didn't we? These alleys are ours.'

That was my Bilal. That was why I loved him.

After that it became a nightly game. I waited around to spot Bilal as he set off on his hunt. He'd choose a new route every day, ambush a new patrol. None of his attacks caused any real harm—a broken windshield here, a spilled plate of food there. One unsuspecting victim bent over to pick up something from the road just when Bilal let go of his shot, and ended up swearing and clutching a severely bruised bottom.

They became smarter soon enough, and started hunting him, coordinating patrols, and putting more men in the patrols. In the day the army and police began walking around Chhote Qazipur, harassing any young man they saw, and slowly news spread that there was a defender of the mohalla's honour. Chhote Qazipur suddenly found a hero, a masked phantom of the night.

But Bilal was pushing his luck. As usual, he was alone. People were happy to accept his heroics, but would not take a risk to help him. As usual, he was generous and didn't care, as usual he was reckless and I knew he'd get caught. Of all the people who had been his gang, only I still stayed by him.

I'd growl if there was a sudden patrol, nudge him softly if I heard something he hadn't. With our knowledge of the streets and my sharp senses we held out until the fateful evening they cornered us.

They hunted us down like the shikaris used to chase a tiger out of a forest. It was a beat.

As soon as Bilal's marble shattered a windshield that night, sirens went off across Chhote Qazipur. Trucks pushed into narrow alleys where only scooters should have gone. A dozen patrols chased us through the streets, but Bilal laughed like a madman and pelted down the narrow lanes, jumping over half-built walls, and dashing through abandoned houses that only the residents of Chhote Qazipur knew.

Then, just one street from his house, he was caught. Almost.

There were three of them standing in the middle of the road. Just behind them was a low wall. And behind that was the gali of Bilal's home. All he needed was to get past the three soldiers.

There was only one thing to do. I jumped in front of him, hoping to be a distraction, barking madly.

'Silence the dog!' one of the soldiers yelled. 'Do it or we will.'

'Silence *him*?' I heard Bilal's muffled voice behind me. Then I felt his hands grasp my hind legs.

DAGGER IN THE EAST

You've heard of the hanging of Jalali sahib, the hanging that did not happen? Of course you have, you are from Mirzapur, it is a legend there, how he went to his hanging and came back atop an elephant at the head of a parade, with drums and singing, of people so delirious in happiness, dogs barking before them, that the women of his household thought it was a mob come to ransack their home and fled—wailing—to seek shelter in the neighbourhood mosque.

That is how the story is told, how the former jailor of the Raj went to his death and came back a hero, a saviour of the people. Excuse me if this dog chooses not to believe the old tale.

Oh, I have no doubt he was there, in his starched white kurta pyjama, the only adornments on his person being the doshala wrapped around his body and the single gold ring on his left hand. These would be the executioner's due, to be taken off the corpse of the man he hanged cleanly, swiftly, so that the body fell sharply enough to break the neck and there was no indignity of thrashing and choking, of kicking legs, or, god forbid, soiled pyjamas.

As part of the elite, of the shurfa, this much was given to Jalali sahib—to bribe the executioner. The Angrez had left only that much of the dignity of the city intact, even after the blood and rebellion of 1857, the battles and defeat, the Sikhs and Gurkhas in the Company forces taking their revenge on Gorakhpur for earlier wars, now that the tables were turned.

It had been two years since the city fell, and the hangings had not stopped. Lowborn, highborn, and even those of unknown parentage, none was spared by the Angrez. Some were buried, some cremated, some left for the dogs who were the true victors, feasting on human flesh—exclusively native now, but in the early days of the uprising, on imported flesh as well.

Jalali sahib was merely the most prestigious of

those being hanged that day; a dozen others waited their turn. Few of them could afford a doshala, and the rings that adorned their hands were made of brass or copper. No hangman would care for those, so they could expect no special consideration. Nonetheless, they preserved their dignity as well as they could.

None of them had eaten for a day, a few had fasted for longer than that. The Angrez had offered them a last meal of their choice, and it had seemed like unusual cruelty to the men who knew they would lose control of their bowels upon the rope. They had refused, all of them, surviving on water in their cells as they contemplated their hollow-eyed end, a prayer on their lips to Allah, Rama, Krishna, Kali. Even the Buddha's name was repeated end on end by some of them.

'It will be all right,' Jalali sahib had said as his name was called. And they had taken heart at that. The drowning will clutch even a straw, and this was a man of weight. Despite his slim build, his bony physique that was neither tall nor short, Jalali sahib's soft voice had power. It was not just that he was a notable of the city, for the zamindars were despised as much as they were respected; it was that the whole city remembered how he had opened the jail doors that summer of 1857 to let out each and every person held under the whip of the Angrez, almost all of them for failure or refusal to pay taxes—the only real crime that had been recognised over the last few decades had been failure to fill John Company's coffers, or to raise voice or fist against the exorbitant tax.

And it was for this deed that he would be hanged. The only mystery was why his turn had come so late. It had been two whole years of hangings at the great tree by the Jama Masjid, whole families had been left with mere boys, none older than ten or twelve, as the supposed heads of families. Now, finally, the time had come, and Jalali sahib made his way to his doom, a guard on his left, a guard on his right, his head held steady, his pace dignified.

They say it was exactly at this moment that the rider came, all the way from Awadh, carrying news of the Angrez queen's mercy. Victoria, adorned with the Kohinoor that the Purabias had only recently wrested from the divided Sikhs—who, incidentally, were in the forefront of the Angrez armies that marched on Gorakhpur—had been overcome with mercy for her rebellious subjects. Now that the aged Mughal,

Bahadur Shah, had been exiled to Rangoon, after the heads of his sons had been placed before him on a platter; now that the treasuries had been looted, and rebels executed or sent to penal colonies in the islands beyond the seas, pity had filled the regal bosom and a pardon was issued in her name.

This, it is said, was the news that the rider came carrying that morning, and as Jalali ascended the steps to his doom, he was told he was free to go. Without a stumble or a stutter, as if he had been told his naashta was ready, he turned to the rest of the prisoners waiting behind him and declared, 'Your lives are your own.'

It took them a moment to process the news, and then, when the guards did not club down Jalali sahib for this declaration, hope arose among them in sighs, in chatter, building up to a roar. Where they found the elephant, nobody knows, but it was on elephant back that Jalali sahib rode back home, a conqueror, a saviour, a jailor who had opened the door again, and how!

This is what we are told, and it sounds plausible enough, if you do not look too closely. Because when you do, you would have to ask about that rider, his timing, the gullibility of the prisoners. And above everything else, the silence of the Angrez. In this whole fairytale, they never speak, and anybody who knows anything about the firangis knows that they never shut up, and insert themselves into any and every story, claiming it as their own, for Queen and country, or God and King, or whatever name greed is dressed up in whatever age.

The Angrez had crushed the uprising with cannons and steel, aided by allies old and new, but more than anything else, they had crushed it using rail and telegram. While the rebels passed messages hidden in cooked rotis marked with blood and spit, the Angrez communicated through their metal wires, sent their battalions rattling around the country in their iron carts racing on shining steel rails. So why did the message of amnesty from the Queen of half the world, a news of such import, come with a rider from Awadh, a lone man on a tired horse?

And how could such a message be kept secret? After so many deaths, after such a war, after all the massacres, how could it be that nobody anywhere else heard of this miraculous chance at life, or if anybody did, not a word was whispered of it in a land desperate for any reprieve at all? Are we to believe that all those men and women who had made themselves what they were by hanging on to each and every word of the Angrez, who had bribed and seduced, who had flattered and killed just for access to the smallest bit of news, were taken by surprise? Or that they knew of something so momentous and did not seek to make use of it? That would have been a first! A desi who saw an opportunity and did not enrich himself, or use it to tear down his neighbour? Such a thing was unheard of while the sun never set on the Empire, and it's been unheard of since.

Then there is the mystery of the silent Angrez, why did they not announce the amnesty in the name of their fat Queen, why did they not dress her in looted glory, hang mercy upon her brow as the Kohinoor dangled upon her neck? Why did they let Jalali sahib claim that grace?

And the men sentenced to be hanged, suddenly free, are we to believe that their fasting, their fear, had made them lose their senses? That in Jalali sahib's words they saw their prayers—to their gods, to their prophets, to their saints—had come true? These were rebels, maybe not the pick of them, maybe only the dregs of them, but these were battle-hardened men with some pride, who had seen the ruthlessness of the Angrez, their brutality, and accepted their fate and vowed not to let their sphincters unclench with death. Are we to believe that they were so gullible that they would make a hero out of a man, helpless as themselves, without asking why or how?

And the elephant, again—where did that elephant come from? And the dogs that ran before it, barking, yowling, what was it that they said? They were my forefathers, they couldn't have been fools.

Ah, no, we are not so easily misled here in the land of the Rapti and Ghagra, we have seen empires come and go, we have seen kings crowned and hanged.

There's another story I've heard, a rushing river of a story with many little tributaries and eddies and waterfalls and it may confuse you, but there's something in it, a richness, some magic, some bewilderment, that does justice to our land. Naturally, that's the story I'm inclined to believe.

But I smell kachoris. Pandey has set up his stall. You'll need to excuse me.

As I was saying, there's another story I've heard of the hanging that was not. And it has to do with a

Power in this land, the treasure that the Purab, the East, guards and will not give away. And because of what happened after the hanging that wasn't.

Jalali sahib went quickly into exile with all his family—not far away to Arabia, as many did, across dreaded sea and inhospitable desert, but to Indore, to the court of the Holkars, where he was treated with dignity and honour, for it is whispered that he gave away a secret, and kept it too, and in the Purab, a certain Power still resides, untouchable, unclaimable. And the Holkars, allies though they were of the Angrez, understood that they owed a greater loyalty to something that needed to be guarded and could not be given away.

It is an old legend, older, they say, than the shards of pottery that you can still find from the empire that gave birth to the woman who would give birth to Gautama, who would be called the Buddha. Do you wonder why he, the Enlightened One, at whose feet it is said the gods rained flowers, came to our backyard for his release from samsara and rebirth? Do you wonder why the Mahavira passed this way on his journey to Pawapuri for his nirvana? Why Gorakhnath found himself in this corner of the wide world, or why Nanak came all the way here to engage in debate with the yogis, or why Kabir chose Maghar, a stone's throw away, to teach against dead rituals, a lesson your people still have not understood?

There is something to the mitti here, the soil itself, pliant and fertile; it harbours rebellion against grand human endeavours, and breeds insurgency. This mitti has drawn saint and martyr and rogue, all those who reject the leash, even of the cycle of birth and death.

Ever and always imperial Dilli has had its eyes on our corner of Hindustan—the Purab, the East, by another name—and reached out with its long arm to claim this land, only to lose it, and lose it again. More than seven hundred years ago, the Tughlaqs sent a governor to rule in their name, only for a new Sultanate to rise in the area, called Sharqi, and threaten Dilli itself. The Lodis finally smashed that new power, but even they had been taught to fear the rebelliousness of the East.

Centuries later, when Akbar eased himself into the throne, with scheming and war, bloody handed and indomitable, the East rose in rebellion, once, twice, thrice. Akbar rode forth, his general Todar Mal rode forth, Jaunpur was captured, and in Gorakhpur too the rebels briefly bowed their necks—only to rise in rebellion again, disappearing, when pursued, into the forests that stretched for hundreds of miles around Gorakhpur. And it was whispered then—and you know the court of Akbar was a court of storytellers and gossips—that something was buried there, something of the soil itself, the rebellious heart of the Purab made manifest. It was whispered that somewhere in the East, this Purab, there existed a short dagger of inconspicuous make but with a stone upon its hilt that looked blue in the sun and glinted red as blood in moonlight. It was said that it was Kush, son of proud Sita, who had breathed into the jewel his rebellion against his father, Rama, and that those in the forests of Purab who had ever found and held the dagger would always rise against mighty cities and empires.

Who knows what Akbar made of that story? Who knows if that is why he gave his firman that anyone who cleared any part of the forests could claim the land as his own; or if that was the reason he plied the region with aid and grants and sought to buy it to his side?

He tried, the great Mughal. But the rebellion never truly died out, not in this halfway land, this region of dacoits and free people, of men with sharp blades, and women too sharp to even need one.

Uprising after uprising in the East forced the Mughals to respond, and generations later, Moazzam Shah, great-great grandson of Akbar, the eldest progeny of the dour Aurangzeb, rode out to these lands. The royal proclamation was that he came not for war but shikar—although it wasn't said whether of men or beasts. As became a prince of the realm, the shikar involved hundreds of soldiers, Turcomen and Pathans, Persian cavalry and Mewari infantry. There were elephants, hunting dogs and guns. Huge tents were pitched around the old abaadi of Gorakhpur, that bend in the land around which the river waters of the Rapti flowed, the prince's camp held in the palm of an earthen hand.

Moazzam Shah found his shikar—masses of it, including, it is said, a tiger so royal that he could not bear to see it killed. That day he turned away his elephants, with two great beasts mauled so badly by the king of the jungle that they were scarcely fit enough to flee, and decided to leave, having found and captured some rebels to soothe his father's prickly pride. But some of Moazzam Shah's soldiers stayed, having become used to the land, its fertile fields, its forests and mists, adding bits to the city here or there, like Turkman Gate, until, like so many visiting gods, humans, dogs and birds before them, they too were swallowed by the land.

And then came the termites, the white ants of the known world: John Company, chewing away at one principality after another. The high priests of treachery. Using war where money and deceit could not work, they had started to gain their petty enclaves and little areas of influence. They'd had their spies in the Mughal court since the days of Aurangzeb, and they had heard of Moazzam Shah's spectacular shikar around Gorakhpur; of the mile upon mile of forest land and fertile land. And they'd heard whispers, too, about a mysterious dagger with a jewel that glinted one colour during the day and another at night.

It took them time to get there, though; centuries. It was only in 1801 that Gorakhpur was ceded to British rule by the Nawab of Awadh, Asaf ud Daula, but like so many imperial rulers before them, they found only little profit here and great rebellion. The revenues from the indigo plantations paid less than the cost of subduing the fierce Banjaras of the forests.

And then, suddenly, the Gorkhas intervened.

The Gorkhas of Nepal had claimed sovereignty over our forests for decades, but had not ruled these parts at all. Now they became active.

It was the year 1805, the Raja of Butwal, that shifty settlement between the hills of Nepal and the plains of Hindustan, was imprisoned by the Angrez on the excuse of not paying his dues, and interrogated. Perhaps they thought he knew the secret hidden from them—the secret of the dagger, the source of the strange, improbable power of the East, our Purab Desh. And perhaps the Gorkhas believed this too, and suspected that the Butwal Raja would conspire with the Angrez to rob them of these lands that they had never bothered to rule—as if they could have, even had they tried! Immediately upon his release by the British, the Raja was captured by the Gorkhas and taken to Nepal, where he died mysteriously in jail.

This was the beginning of a series of skirmishes leading eventually to a full-blown war, and the subjugation of the Gorkhas to British rule. In just a decade, the Gorkhas turned from the most recalcitrant of rebels into the most willing soldiers of the British Empire, as if some mysterious force had been lost to them.

Whatever it was, the wily Angrez did not gain from their victory, and a few decades later Gorakhpur was as unruly as ever. A rash of small insurrections erupted in Purab Desh, and they would soon gather force and come together in the great Uprising of 1857. Gorakhpur, at the centre of these insurgencies, was administered by an Angrez Joint Magistrate named Bird, and he found that his exalted chair was not the most comfortable of perches. There was rumour of an insurrection in neighbouring Azamgarh as well, and worse further afield.

During these troubled times, a British civil surgeon, travelling from Gorakhpur to Azamgarh, found his troop besieged by a sullen mob on the road. Hurrying their mounts, they reached Jaunpur, where they begged shelter at the haveli of the nobleman Mohammed Hassan, and Hassan gave them refuge.

As the mob gathered before his gate, as flaming torches were brought out and slogans hurled against the Angrez and the haveli, Mohammed Hassan had the Angrez dressed in native clothes and hustled out the rear entrance. The mob remained at Hassan's gate till late into the night, but they did not have the courage to take him on, and by that time the Civil

Surgeon was halfway to Benares, from where he would send a note about his troubles and his rescuer to Bird.

Meanwhile, Bird himself had been feeling more and more besieged. He was not sure how many troops would stay loyal to him and wondered—if he commanded them to fire on the natives, would they turn their guns on him instead? The great Uprising of 1857 was yet to happen, but murmurs of a rebellion already filled the air. When he received the note from the Civil Surgeon it was as if it was a sign from the heavens and he wrote to Mohammed Hassan asking if he would take over the administration of Gorakhpur, while Bird himself repaired to climes more favourable to his countrymen.

Mohammed Hassan agreed, and gathering a troop of trusted advisors and a small band of strangers, started for Gorakhpur. But in Gorakhpur itself, things had changed—the soil, after all, is slippery, and here, more than in any place on earth, do the plans of mice and men go oft astray. People whispered to Bird that maybe Hassan was not what he portrayed himself to be. Yes, he had saved the Angrez, but that was a matter of honour, because nobility does not dismiss a plea for refuge, but where did his loyalties truly lie? Jaunpur was the heart of the old Sharqi dynasty, the rebellious dynasty of Purab Desh that had sent elephants to the gates of Dilli itself. Hassan might give his allegiance to the Nawab of Awadh, but maybe he felt entitled to rule himself? What if he came to Gorakhpur and then never left? Bird, confused by the currents of a land that he could still not understand, surrounded on all sides by news of insurrection, decided to ambush the very man he had invited to relieve him of his duties as the sahib, the mai-baap of Gorakhpur.

As Bird marshalled his forces, Mohammed Hassan's small troop camped in the forests. Their force was a small one, lightly armed, prepared for peace, and the arms only a show of force as an alibi for Bird, so that he would be spared the fury of *his own* mai-baap for abandoning his post. They would not have known what fate awaited them.

And yet they met somebody in the forests that changed everything. They were given news, and they were given something else. They say a Banjara came from the depths of the forest, a dog on his left and a dog on his right—neither related to me, I make no claims—and he offered Hassan a knife. The

Banjara did not speak, he did not bow. He stood tall and imperious before a nobleman, and Mohammed Hassan, proud as he was, kneeled to accept the dagger that glinted red in the night.

The next day Bird's forces sprang forth from their ambush, and though they outnumbered Hassan's men three times over, they were routed. Bird himself fled into the forests, blind with panic, and spent days in the treacherous landscape until he emerged near Patna, hundreds of miles away, run ragged with terror. In Gorakhpur Hassan assembled the leaders, foremost among them Bandhu Singh. Shoulder to shoulder they stood, and announced that Gorakhpur was free once again, a liberated city, in a region proud of its freedom. Far away, the aged Mughal Emperor, Bahadur Shah Zafar, heard the call, and sent his trusted man, Musharraf Khan, to travel five hundred miles to this rebel enclave that would enjoy its freedom, even if briefly.

As India rose, and the Angrez were slaughtered, fleeing battlefields everywhere, Gorakhpur returned to what it was, a land wreathed in mists, a quiet place of a few tens of thousands of inhabitants. For a year and a day, Mohammed Hassan ruled, with Bandhu

Singh by his side. Every day that Hassan sat in his court, he placed before him a dagger, plain in design except for an ornamental stone of curious design.

And then Dilli fell, and Awadh fell, and the armies of the Angrez, with the Gorkhas at their right hand and the Sikhs at their left, arrived at Gorakhpur, and even this little enclave fell.

Where did it go, that jewelled weapon, in that final fall? Nobody knew, nobody spoke of it. Then two years later, Jalali sahib, ascending the platform for the hanging that was not to be, said, 'I know of the dagger.'

At these words everything was stayed. There was a messenger on horseback, all right, but he *left* the hanging ground, did not *come* to it, and at a nod from the Angrez, Jalali sahib turned to the condemned men and told them that this was not the day that they were going to die.

The telegram raced from Gorakhpur to Dilli, to Kalkatta, to Vilayat across the oceans, and an amnesty was declared while the soldiers of the Angrez searched the forest fifteen miles from Gorakhpur, near a place called Rajoura, the site of a crumbling Gorkhali fortress. And one soldier was seized of fever and died, and another, then another. Their brains swelled, their bodies racked with fever, they bled through their noses and ears, and they died.

The Angrez doctors thought it might be mosquitoes, or a mite, or a type of shrub grass. They called it acute encephalitis syndrome. Fancy words that changed nothing. The searches ground to a halt, were resumed, and abandoned again.

In Indore, it is said, Jalali sahib read about this in the newspaper, turned it over, and had another cup of tea.

What was it that he had revealed after he was spared the gallows, and what was it that he had withheld? Nobody knew, though it is said that his blood carries the truth among his descendants to this day. But whatever he said, whatever the Angrez heard, could have had no meaning. You cannot give away rebellion, no matter what emperor, no matter what queen, reaches out to claim it as their own. Even the Buddha, the Enlightened One, learned that the truth of life could only be embraced by giving up his throne.

That is the story of Jalali sahib's non-hanging, his escape and exile. Or the version I choose to believe.

It is only a small part of a larger story, though, and Jalali sahib's role was only a cameo, a part with only a few whispered words that only the sharp ears of a stray dog might have heard. The story began long before him, and continues long after him.

You will have heard that sixty years after the hanging that did not happen, Gandhi arrived in Gorakhpur on a train. A horse-drawn carriage was sent to him by the government prosecutor, but the crowds removed the horse, and drew the carriage to the maidan upon their shoulders. Thousands were present to hear Gandhi speak. It was the largest crowd he had ever addressed. After he spoke, an arm was raised, a dark arm of a man from the forest, standing free in that crush of bodies, with a dog on his right and another on his left, and his hand held a dagger. There are people who say that 'Mahatma' was only one title that was cried out. Another title too was raised. 'Maharaj, Purab ka Maharaj'. The King of the East—the king of all the east, and the king of our Purab Desh.

Gandhi left Gorakhpur, stunned and moved by the reception. The rebellion he had sown found ready soil, not so the idea that rebellion must be peaceful.

The Banjaras gathered in the dusk, and one of their own showed a sign that the others recognised as it glinted red. They bowed to the man who held the sign, called him king, King of the East. He led them forth to battle, and the policemen, Angrez and their willing slaves, who used their might so freely, cowered and died in the fire of Chauri Chaura.

I could tell you of other days when the dagger shone blue and nights when it shone red and things happened. But let me tell you only of one, so recent you'd remember it well.

You will have heard of a hospital, of the paediatric doctor in charge of the encephalitis ward, of the oxygen supply being cut, of the deaths, of the government's frenzy against a man who tried to save dying children. And some said that it was because he was Muslim, and maybe that was the reason. But maybe it was not, because it is said that in his time in jail he was interrogated. He was asked, "Was your grandmother a Jalali? What is your relation to Indore?"

'I just tried to save the children,' he said.

What of the dagger, he was asked. Of the dagger he did not know, and they tried for many days but he did not know, and so, finally, he was let go, but into exile, though not to Indore.

They say that the only man who knows of the dagger, who holds it and bestows its power on the chosen ones, is still out there. The King of the East, somewhere in the forests of our Purab. Although there are others who say he is everywhere. They say that his kingdom is freedom, that it cannot be wrested away, that his lineage is long, and not of blood but rebellions. They say there is such a king, still, in India, and he waits for his day, to rise once again.

THE BUDDHA'S SMILE

They met at the railway station, Carnegie King and Knownto Sharma, in Gorakhpur, which boasted the longest railway platform in India, in the world maybe, although India has changed, and the world too, since those days, and you can boast about anything and somebody will provide you the photos to prove it.

But the pictures are all digital now, all tricks of the light, an illusion of the eye. Back then, in the early '80s, we still held the physicality of the proof of images, a photograph was a real thing, however blurry or unclear, it was something real.

The railway station was still the biggest thing in

Gorakhpur. The airport was only for the Air Force and the odd Vayudoot flight from Lucknow used by the very important few; it was not the overpacked terminal it is now, ferrying labour to the South, to the Gulf, and wherever else they can flee to earn some money. The Bihari politicians hadn't yet wrested the rail ministry away, and with that the contracts, the mafia and everything else. You aren't old enough, so you won't understand that the railway station was everything in Gorakhpur, the heart and liver and spine of this city.

Everyone travelled in and out by train. There were the buses, of course, but the less said about them the better. Dogs were probably allowed to hop onto them, but I never tried, so I don't know the worst of it, but there are things I've heard. There is the tale of the lady who, choking on the foetid air inside, valiantly pushed open her jammed window a crack, against the advice of her fellow passenger, and was rewarded with a face full of gobar. It was the third day of Holi, and colour and water were in short supply.

And the world came to our railway station, even if it was a brief stopover on the way to Nepal, or to get on the Buddhist circuit, or even to take a break from the long journey from Jammu in the west to Bengal in the east. Day and night the trains came and stopped, disgorging and swallowing vast numbers of bodies like great monsters, their mournful horns like the mating calls of lonely beasts echoing across the land, their arrival always announced by the forced cheeriness of the automated message saying how late they were, and how much it was regretted.

Always and ever the station heaved with bodies, it was the place of a thousand shouted cries, and a million silent crimes and happy transgressions, although the pace slowed down as night gathered, and came to a crawl around two in the night, before slowly starting up again. Though even then, no matter how late it was, there was the criminal and the prey, and occasionally the police and the fool, like in the case of Qazi Shafiullah sahib who, convinced that charity could only be truly done if the recipient did not know who did the deed, and would therefore only praise God in his ignorance, was creeping about one night with blankets under his arms, sneakily inserting them under the heads of poor men and women asleep on the platform. He even had the occasional blanket for a dog on a winter's foggy night.

It soothed Shafiullah Sahib's mind, this ritual of charity. Until the night he was caught in the act by a sharp-eyed constable, who had watched the shadowy figure flit from one unsuspecting sleeping form to another. A man as proud of his waxed moustache as of his well-earned cynicism, Ram Kumar was sure that the shaking man in his grasp was guilty of something, for who would attempt something as monumentally stupid as doing a good deed, night after night, on that platform of woes.

It was Knownto who had intervened, who knew both the constable and the fallen noble, and had the right words to say, and was rewarded by both in their separate ways.

Knownto Sharma would never have been caught so unawares as Shafiullah Sahib had been. In fact, he had never been caught at all. It was part of his fame, the reason why he was a legend in his own right, with two names that were both lies.

The first name was, of course, merely a title, a crown of respect awarded to him by his admirers, his victims, and all those in the vast circle of people who had fallen—even briefly—under the shadow of the most notable pickpocket to operate on the NER, the North Eastern Railways. He was famous, known to all, and Knownto he was called.

The Sharma was more complicated. Knownto claimed no family, and thus no caste, but there is no escaping such a label, whether you claim it or not. He was anointed a Brahmin sometime in his late teens—possibly by a policeman who later realised that he had been bribed with money taken out of his own wallet. It was a title given in both respect and derision, and not a little fear. Maybe people who had been so soundly duped needed to believe that the man who had performed such a feat needed to be preternaturally crafty, and since the only way they could relate to this was by caste, a Sharma he was called.

Not that Knownto acknowledged any of this, not his first name or the last. He certainly wore no caste mark, and if he wore a sacred thread across his body, nobody had seen it poking out from under the flowered shirts he favoured, the first two buttons open, revealing, in the summers, the shining white of his baniyaan and a peculiar little locket made of some unidentifiable metal that glinted this colour and that.

All that Knownto Sharma did when either of the

two names was taken, with the "ji" attached, was raise an eyebrow, or let the delicate nostrils at the end of his aquiline nose flare ever so slightly. It was both acknowledgement and dismissal from the undisputed master of the quick touch, the faint flutter, and the thousand little twists and turns that differentiate a true master from a mere wannabe. Even those who feared his silent, invisible raid on their purse and pocket were in awe of him.

He was supreme, never bested, an artist with no rival.

Until he met Carnegie King. The firangi who not only bested Knownto Sharma, he made Knownto do the job of deceiving himself.

'Always dump the wallet', is the first commandment that a successful pickpocket follows. The wallet, or purse, is irrelevant, the money inside is all that matters. Wallets and purses were singular, recognisable, money was anonymous, and free—once it had been successfully extracted from those too unwary to deserve the keeping of it.

But when the thief's code is well known, it is his own trap. Anything that is set in stone is a stumbling block. Knownto may not have read Sun Tzu, but he had learned the great maxim of war that the Chinese strategist had taught so long ago: the essence of success in battle is surprise. Be where you are not expected, and never be where you are expected to be.

And yet the gora fooled him, for Carnegie King went one step further—he changed what was expected, changed the landscape on which the battle was fought. Five feet away from the garbage bin where he had so quickly discarded King's wallet for the trash it was, Knownto came to a sudden halt, holding in his hand the only thing that had been in the wallet: a playing card with the king of diamonds jeering at him.

Never had he been so surprised, stopped in midstride. And now he felt a hand drop on his shoulder, and heard an unfamiliar, curious voice say to him jovially, 'I see that you got my card, Sharma ji.'

Knownto turned to look at this man who had him in his grip. He was like no gora that Knownto had ever encountered. In fact, it is fair to say, that the likes of Carnegie King had never been seen in Gorakhpur before, and have not been seen since. And Gorakhpur had seen a lot of goras. It was, after all, the first part of Awadh that the East India Company had latched on to. This was where the goras set up their indigo plantations, their opium farms and later, their snooty Railway colony.

For two centuries they had come and gone, until all that was now left was a trickle of hippies and backpackers wearing atrocious slippers and unseemly clothes. Yes, there was a posh gora now and then, travelling with the family on the Buddha trail, or enroute to Nepal—some oddity who chose not to fly from Delhi to Kathmandu, avoiding the muddy, polluted sea of humanity that was the Gangetic Plain for the pristine beauty of the Himalayas where they could dump their expensive trash and pollute the very roof of the world—but this was rare.

And somebody like King was unheard of.

Partly it was the man himself. He had the peculiar blocky solidity that some Americans have, as if they've been carved whole from an old oak, their muscles not so much cords as flat slabs. This impression was heightened by Carnegie's square, and outsized, head. Even though he was a couple of inches under six feet—not very tall for America, but substantially so for Gorakhpur—the sheer physicality of the man took up so much space that people automatically took a step back. Given that this was an Indian railway station, and one of the biggest, this meant that as Carnegie King walked through the platform, people stumbled over others to avoid him. Small quarrels erupted as toes and whole feet were stepped upon. King moved in an inviolate bubble.

As if this weren't intimidating enough, King also had the smile of a tiger—large, feral, and amused at something that the person on the receiving end knew was going to be at his or her expense. And he *looked* at people, truly looked at them, saw them whole, totted up their totals, and came to a measurement, an assessment in his head. It was not the sly genius of whores or ticket examiners, who know exactly the amount to charge a customer or just the right bribe to ask for a berth in an overfull train compartment. Those calculations, as cold and mercenary as they were, still implied a relationship. King's eyes had none of that, there was no room for any familiarity. He was observing, cataloguing, and you were only the current specimen under his microscope.

This was how Knownto felt when the big man laid a hand on his shoulder, pulled him close, and spoke in his hideously accented but perfectly understandable Hindi. Somehow, Knownto felt certain that even if the man had spoken in some foreign tongue, like Swahili or Gujarati, he would not have dared to misunderstand him.

'I am looking for a man,' Carnegie King said, the words, the compulsion, searing themselves into Knownto's head, 'and I am told you are the one person who can find anybody you want to.'

After a pause, he added, 'His name is Gangu Ram.'

Knownto's shrug was eloquent. It said in a gesture what in words might have been, 'If you shake any tree in a fifty-mile radius, a Gangu Ram or two will fall from it. The name is so common that if you shake a jamun tree really hard, you will find more Gangu Rams than fruit lying on the ground.'

King understood Knownto's shrug precisely, to the last word, and added, 'He is the younger brother of Hukum Singh, the shikari.'

This invited no shrug, but a sharp intake of breath, and Knownto Sharma finally spoke.

'You do not seek a man, sir, you seek a legend,' he said.

The broad tiger's smile on King's face became deeper and wider, hungrier. 'That is why I have you, my friend, that is why I have you.'

But here Carnegie King was wrong, or not entirely right; it was a mistake of languages. Words mean different things in different languages, and when Knownto said 'legendary', what he meant was closer to 'mythical'. And for all the force of his personality, even Carnegie King could not turn one thing to the other.

Gangu Ram was an icon, a figure of such renown that no physical reality could really encompass him. People had told his story for half a century, but had not seen him for decades. Everybody knew *of* him, but none knew him. Like a tiger in the forest—his presence was everywhere and overwhelming, but the lord of the jungle himself could not actually be seen.

Gangu Ram's story begins with a White memsahib, but not the kind you would expect, not some Angrez officer's wife terrified as much of the Indian sun as of Indian men. It is said that barely a year before the British Raj fell, torn away like some massive spiderweb that had looked enormous but had been insubstantial in the end, a big-boned American woman had come to Hindustan looking to kill a tiger. She had tried in one princely state after another, and somehow always missed her chance. With World War II over, and the preparations of British departure clear to all and sundry, she became desperate. Desperate to have the thrill of the fabled shikar that so many had sought in this land which would surely plunge into chaos and barbarism the instant that White rule ended. She may never be able to come here again.

Someone told her she should try in Bahraich, she couldn't fail there. But she did; the tigers refused to be seen, much less shot.

Close to psychological collapse, she finally came to Gorakhpur, to try and find Hukum Singh, the man she was told had guided more than a hundred hunters, the old ghost of the forest who could sniff the air and tell which direction a tiger had taken, and what was more, whether it was male or female. She offered the princely sum of a thousand rupees, an astronomical amount, enough to turn a poor man into a petty raja.

What the American lady did not know was that the man whom she offered the small fortune to was not Hukum Singh, but his ne'er-do-well younger brother, Gangu Ram.

It was an innocent mistake. Hukum Singh had caught a fever. The Angrezi doctor was perplexed, the hakims and vaids too. As the disease, whatever it may have been, ravaged his large frame, stealing the vitality for which he had always been so well known, they found that they could prescribe little but rest, meals of gruel-like khichdi, and a caution against the curse of the envious.

Gangu Ram had come to the American memsahib to apologise on his brother's behalf and convey his regrets, but seeing his dour countenance, and knowing refusal was around the corner, she exclaimed, 'A thousand rupees, Hukum Singh, I will give you a thousand rupees!'

The sum was so outrageous that the spectators—a number of whom knew that it was Gangu Ram not Hukum Singh who stood before the mem—were struck dumb. Gangu Ram spluttered, coughed, and then said, 'Thursday, Thursday, it is a good day.' It would give him four days' time.

He would try to explain to his brother later that evening, and Hukum Singh would listen with compassion. He had never scorned his younger brother, and known that some of the reputation for fecklessness was unearned. Part of it was even his, Hukum Singh's, fault. Large trees steal the wealth around them, and only puny runts grow nearby.

'It has been said,' he whispered softly, 'so it must be done.'

And then they discussed how. It was not magic, nor some god-given gift of smell, that had made Hukum Singh the shikari he was, but jungle-craft; hours and days of patiently observing the habits of all living creatures, years that had become decades of walking in the forests, among the chatter of monkeys, the many and various calls of the birds, the startled bark of deer and the carefully choreographed tapping of their feet. He could look at a pug mark in the soft earth and estimate the age of the tiger from its width, guess its size by the length of its stride, figure out how long it had passed that way by observing the crumbling of the soil at the edges.

Some of this Gangu Ram had picked up, but it was nowhere near the skill needed to track a tiger in the forest. That way lay death, or a severe mauling. But fate had presented them with a chance. A cattle lifter had been operating near the village of Morai close to Padri Bazar. A beast that risked hunting so close to human habitation might be old or injured. This would make it both easy prey as well as a danger that needed to be eliminated before it moved from a diet of cattle to that of the people who herded them.

Gangu Ram left the next day, arriving while the sun was climbing, determined to do his scouting while light was in the sky. He carried his brother's twelve-bore shotgun, but that was a gun for duck or deer, not big game. At best it would startle a tiger, at worst, an injury would drive the animal into a killing rage. Gangu Ram prayed only for some sign, and desperately hoped to avoid an encounter.

The villagers did not know that, and the laws of the goras being what they were, they had rarely seen an Indian with a gun. This transformed Gangu Ram instantly into a valiant hunter—and one of their own!—and they crowded around him as he asked how many cattle they had lost, and where.

As much from a sense of shame as anything else, he decided to do the stalking alone. A calf had been killed six days ago, and after they showed him from where it had been taken, a plot of land bordering the forest, he bade the villagers to stay at home, and swung on in. A dog from the village followed him, but only to the edge of the forest.

This was not dense jungle, but nor was it just

brush. There was enough water in these parts for trees and thick undergrowth, but the soil was sandy in parts, leading to wide stretches of open space, and trails made by human feet and bullock carts over decades. It was along one of these trails, just past a glade, that Gangu Ram saw his first set of pug marks.

He squatted down to take a closer look at one pug mark, and was astonished at the size. It looked as big as a dinner thali. This was a tiger, all right, not a dainty leopard. As he sat and pondered, a stray breeze cooled his sweat, and he saw the sandy soil crumble ever so slightly at the edges of the dinner plate.

Suddenly the overwhelming sound of insects that had been all around him was blanked out. His head felt like a hot, overlarge balloon, the terror was enormous, filling him up, and his sense of self was so insignificant. Because one thing that Gangu Ram had learned from his brother was that the fresher a pug mark, the sharper were its edges, and if even a breath of wind could make it crumble at the edges, then the tiger had passed this way only half an hour ago, maybe less.

Never a very religious man, Gangu Ram prayed that day, softly, silently, to Durga Ma, She Who

Rode on Tigers, and slowly, as some sanity leaked through the fog of fear, he remembered his brother warning that animals judge a prey by its height. He straightened up, standing as tall as he could, with the shotgun raised like a staff, and turned to walk back to Morai.

He kept his senses, he did not run, even noted a tall tree by the glade that would be excellent for a machan, but his breathing was fast and fierce, the sweat rolling off his body. The jungle was quiet, as if all sound had been pressed down by a giant hand. There was no call of bird or beast. The king was present, and the subjects dare not speak.

At the edge of the jungle, when he could see the fields beyond, he almost ran, but somehow managed to maintain his even pace. He saw the stray dog again, blabbered his fear, and as the words tumbled out, regained some mastery of himself again. He knew he had spent his courage. There was never going to be a time again when he would walk alone into the jungle.

In Morai he talked to the people, gave them instructions, told them where to build the machan, more than twice the height of a man from the ground, bought a goat, and promised to be back in three days to rid them of their cattle thief. He was not a bad man, and warned them not to go into the forest alone, always in groups of four or more, but he was happy to leave, to report to his brother, to tell the crazy American mem that her tiger was there.

They arrived early on the day of the hunt. In the afternoon. The District Collector, the biggest man in town both in power and physical size, accompanied them. There was a daawat, a feast for the villagers and anybody around. The Collector, a middle-aged Englishman married to his job, was nonplussed by the American lady; she did not want a beat, or even a crew, and was going to hunt alone, accompanied by her trusty handmade Holland & Holland .500 Express rifle, and Gangu Ram—whom she referred to still as Hukum Singh.

It all sounded highly inappropriate to the Collector, but he had little experience of women, and none at all of domineering American ones, with riches and power beyond his ken. He mumbled and grumbled, but gave way. Nonetheless, he insisted on accompanying her to the machan, as did all the men and children of the village and some from nearby ones.

A peg was driven into the glade, fifteen feet

from the machan, and the goat—certified to be the champion bleater—tied to it. A ladder was offered for the mem to climb up, while Gangu Ram scrabbled up the tree on his own. There was a large flask of tea, some cups, and a picnic basket, and when all was arranged, the Collector left, the village stray at his heels and the villagers all around him asking about one little piece of paperwork or other. He rarely visited Morai, so for them the audience with him had been gift enough.

It was only an hour or so until dusk, but time moved slowly, it seemed to Gangu Ram. The mem fiddled with her rifle, checked and rechecked her line of sight, ejected and changed the bullets, and then finally felt calm and invincible. Gangu Ram nervously sipped tea; she had been gracious and allowed him to use one of the cups.

Then it was dark, suddenly dark, and the character of the jungle changed. Landmarks that had seemed so clear in the light became blurry, and if you looked too long at any one thing it disappeared from your vision. This is a peculiar affliction of your kind, we dogs do not know of it, but I can guess how that kind of thing would chill your spine. In all of this there was one constant, the sound of the goat chewing grass. It never bleated, and Gangu Ram morosely wondered whether he had been cheated. Or what if the tiger had been upset by all the comings and goings and moved to safer habitat? Or maybe it had killed in another location, was fat and sated, and cared nothing for a single, skinny goat?

He would have failed, would have blackened his brother's name, and come away with nothing.

And then the goat started bleating, and cut his thoughts short. Next to him he felt the mem stiffen, and then slowly stir to extend the rifle, to seek the shadow that stalked the prey.

They had no idea where the tiger was, but the goat knew. Like an iron filing drawn to a magnet, the goat stretched and strained—except in the direction opposite that in which lurked the threat to its life, the direction towards which it alternately lowered and raised its head, bleating, displaying the puny threat of its small horns.

The mem's thumb moved to pull back the hammer, ready now for the kill she had waited for all these weeks, but she was not prepared for the swift, fluid grace of the beast that came suddenly from the forest and pounced. The goat's bleats were cut off as the massive jaws closed around its neck, the sabre-like teeth punching through the vertebrae in the neck, killing it instantly.

And then the mem fired.

The tiger dropped the goat and roared. It was a sound like the ending of the world, booming both from ahead of them and, impossibly, from behind them. As the mem cocked the second hammer, the tiger took one long bound towards the machan, and leaped.

People who have seen tigers only in cages underestimate their size and strength. They think that because the tiger is too heavy an animal to climb, safety lies in the trees. This is true, but only very high up. The villagers had built the machan according to Gangu Ram's instructions, more than twice a tall man's height, about thirteen feet off the ground. It was not high enough.

The tiger got one paw on the machan just as the mem let off her second shot. Terrified, or merely inexperienced, she missed, but so did the tiger. There was the deafening roar of the beast, and the terrifying roar of the rifle at the same moment. The mem fell back on the machan, and the tiger, scrabbling back from the tree, down to earth, shaking it.

But the American mem did not realise she had missed. She had fired straight into that massive beast as it had leapt, and was sure that the second shot had killed him. She got up to peer down at her prize. Gangu Ram lunged forward to stop her, and that is when the tiger made its second leap.

This time it got both of its paws on the machan, and roared straight into the woman's terrified face. Gangu Ram caught her as she fainted dead away, and sat, terrified, the mem prone upon him, as the tiger tried desperately to claw its way on to the machan. He could feel all the tea he had drunk dribbling out of him and soaking his dhoti, but he had no capacity to care.

Again, the tiger fell, again it leaped. Gangu Ram lost count of the number of times this happened, sunk as he was in prayer to Durga Ma, She Who Rode on Tigers, until suddenly he realised that there was no sound, the universe wasn't heaving and shaking. The tiger had left. Leaving them, the machan, even the dead goat, behind.

It took Gangu Ram some moments to come to

his senses, and then he slowly extricated himself from under the mem, wincing as she came to rest on the puddle he had made. Then he undid his dhoti and dried it off as best he could in the feeble breeze, hoping desperately that she would not come awake and catch him in his undergarments. Given what had passed, it should have been the least of his worries, but the thought filled him with horror.

She did not stir, and after letting the breeze dry the cloth for half an hour, Gangu Ram dressed himself again, and revived her with a little splash of cold tea on her face.

She was still terrified when she woke, but after he calmed her down, she realised the shame and ridiculousness of her state, and the overpowering scent of urine that was definitely not of any wild animal.

Gangu Ram was too much of a gentleman to say anything, but he offered to climb higher, on a branch facing away, while she took care of herself with the water that they had. Neither thought of climbing down until the village party, beating drums, having heard the roars and the gunshots, arrived in the morning to retrieve the dead body of the tiger or the bodies of its hunters.

The next day, the mem disappeared, leaving Indian shores forever soon after. But before she left, she had sworn Gangu Ram to silence, paid him five hundred rupees in secret and a thousand in front of half the village. Thus was his legend made.

Hukum Singh laughed long and hard when he was told, whooping, or trying to, as the disease that had him in its grip forced him to cough and struggle. His happiness was large and obvious. Maybe it was because of his undying love for a younger brother. Maybe it was for the tiger that got away—he had spent too many years in the company of people he despised, helping them hunt a beast he admired. Whatever it was, he was delighted in the outcome, and insisted that Gangu Ram keep the money. But the younger brother would not have it, and managed to get Hukum Singh to agree to keep half of it, and even that was a great amount.

But Gangu Ram could not stay. The District Collector did not know exactly what had happened, but he suspected that the people were laughing at the mem's expense. It was intolerable. And the tiger was alive. The British had long ago realised how important the tiger hunt was for them. If local rajas and nawabs saw the contest with the king of the jungle as a mark of their special status, then the British had to outdo them. If Shah Jahan, the Mughal emperor, had hunted half a dozen tigers in carefully cultivated preserves in a year, then the Angrez would hunt hundreds at a go. How better to show the terror and majesty of the Raj than the total and utter devastation it could bring down on local kings—men or animal, it did not matter.

This failed hunt, this joke, the sniggering of peasants, the Collector knew it was something that had to be crushed, especially as British power was teetering so precariously anyway, and to the natives one white person was like another—nobody would believe that the woman who failed to hunt an ageing tiger and was instead rescued by a mere native was not an Angrez. And any attempt to explain otherwise would make matters worse.

Fearing the wrath of the firangis, for he was no fool, Gangu Ram fled to Nepal, and from there to somewhere else, and from somewhere else to somewhere beyond even that. The Collector turned, in his frustration, to Hukum Singh, but in the old shikari he found an opponent beyond his powers.

This was a man revered by the locals and respected by more than a few Angrez shikaris. A good number of the Collector's superiors had nothing but praise for the man who had guided them on their hunts.

Unable to do much directly, the Collector had Gangu Ram declared a criminal absconder, wanted for fraud and unspecified crimes against femininity. Posters went up, but nobody came forward with any information, and if the Collector had wanted to run the man's name down, the opposite happened. The posters sparked conversations, which were further embroidered by fancy, and in the end, Gangu Ram became a mythical half-human-half-tiger hero with whom the most beautiful woman ever born in England—who knew or cared about America?—had eloped.

Then came Independence, and with it the roiling, rolling disaster of Partition. It did not affect Gorakhpur very much. Both halves of Pakistan, east and west, were far away. Shibhan Lal Saxena, who represented Gorakhpur in the Constituent Assembly, was far more interested in leading the fight for democracy against the Nepali state than in the mad Partition. Nonetheless, so great a change could not leave the region entirely untouched. Politics changed, the administration changed, the old posters that bore Gangu Ram's name and description, with a reward of fifty rupees for any information, yellowed and aged, and were blown away. The only thing that remained was the legend of a man who had cheated the empire of a tiger's death and claimed its most beautiful woman.

'He returned, though, this I know, and have confirmed,' Carnegie King said. Knownto did not have the courage to ask how the American knew or who his sources were, but he believed the big man.

They were seated in King's chambers, a vast office space emptied out just for his use at the railway station. It was a thing unheard of, befitting only super senior echelons of management, people who were whispered about but rarely seen. For a gora to have such access bespoke connections and power that Knownto could barely imagine.

'Why?' was the only question Knownto asked.

Again, the American understood the rest of the unspoken question. 'I want to meet Gangu Ram for the secret that Hukum Singh told him, the secret for which I am here, that of the tiger's grass.' And at Knownto's look of incomprehension, the American explained, 'It is known that sometimes tigers will eat grass. It is a phenomenon that has been observed rarely, but it has been seen. We think that it happens when a tiger is ill, has eaten something that does not agree with it, but we do not know which type of grass.'

'Why should it matter?'

'Oh, it matters very much. The tiger is the greatest predator that stalks the earth. Countless aeons of evolution have made it into a killing machine that has few equals, and yet it can be brought to heel by indigestion. This is the genius of India! No other civilisation has devoted so much time and energy to searching for inner peace—in its intestines. Have you read of Gandhi's experiments with the bowels?'

Knownto shook his head. His preferred reading was Ibn Safi's spicy spy novels.

'You must!' Carnegie King exclaimed. 'It is only then you understand how much of India's struggle for freedom was also a struggle against gas and constipation,' he said, his tone deadly serious. 'And it is not a new thing, it has haunted every regime that has ever ruled this place. No other people have spent so much time and energy contemplating what to eat, what not to eat, when to eat it, and why. This is the only country in the world that has churan. There is no word for it in any other language. We do not even understand what it is, whether it is meant to be sweet, or salty, or both, or neither. Everything and anything can be churan, but only a few things are.'

Knownto wondered why the American was telling him all of this. He also realised that it was useless information, it was not some secret he could use for benefit. He had heard it said that a secret is something you can tell another person; a secret that is not betrayed, that is not outed, is of no value. And all this, about tigers and grass and Gandhi and churan, was certainly not worth telling, or even intelligible.

But Knownto could not turn away and leave, of course, refusing to listen to this strange talk. The American had caught him in the act of pickpocketing. He had trapped Knownto Sharma, beaten him at his own game, and this knowledge was like a leash around Knownto's neck, just like that card—the American had refused to take it back—with the king of diamonds, burning like a brand in his shirt pocket.

The American was telling him these things, Knownto felt, because he owned him now. He could say whatever he liked, something top secret or plain rubbish.

'I do not know how long back it goes in history,' Carnegie King continued in his musings, 'and I wonder if it explains the Buddha's smile.'

'The Buddha?' The man's strange talk veered all over the place, and Knownto had to ask not so much to know, for he felt that every step would draw him deeper into confusion, but just to insert a pause into the rush of ideas.

'Yes, the Buddha, the man who was born a prince, who learned that attachment led to suffering, who experienced a situation of such great stillness and peace that he called it Nirvana—no wind—who achieved enlightenment under a tree, and whose smile has never been deciphered. What if it was all about the rich food he was exposed to? What if exercise and fasting gave him no relief, what if he turned back home, to these parts, where his mother comes from—for is it not said that no man is braver than his father, and wiser than his mother?—and found ultimate relief in the grass that the tiger eats?'

'You're mad,' Knownto said, because this was now too much. 'The Buddha was a god, an incarnation of heaven itself. He was not just a man with a stomach ache.'

King laughed. 'Maybe, maybe. But you're an Indian, and I'm an American. You can have your gods and keep them, all I am here for is to find out the secret of the tiger's grass, and for that I need Gangu Ram, and you will find him for me.'

'I will need five hundred rupees,' Knownto said. It was not as big a sum as it had been in the days of Hukum Singh, but it was still a large sum. He did not know why he asked. It was an instinct. Here, in the railway station, built for trade, a temple to trafficking both licit and illicit, the asking and giving of money was almost a prayer, a Hail Mary said at a cathedral.

King did not ask why Knownto needed the money, just laid out five crisp hundred-rupee notes on the table. Then he added another five.

Knownto picked up only five of them, and turned to leave.

'I will wait for you on Thursday,' the American said, and Knownto nodded without turning around, afraid now of the coincidences. A Thursday, four days. Was he being put on the path that Gangu Ram had walked so long ago, to confront a tiger in the forest? But the tiger this time, Knownto knew, was Carnegie King, and no machan, no matter how high, was going to be beyond this one's leap. And there was no American mem with a gun, no thousand rupees, no legend in his future.

With his head whirling, Knownto did a thing that he was rarely known to do. He left the railway station, like a ghost dehoused from his haunt, like a khabees turned away from his place of power.

There was only one place to go, he knew, Baba Tota-Maina ki Kabar, that tiled and shellacked place of glitter just before Gol Ghar, the centre of town. That was the only place where a saint was to be found, and that too a saint tied to tigers.

Knownto knew the story. It was said that for as long as anyone could remember, that place had been nothing but two tumbledown graves, in desperate need of repair. Then a tiger had changed all that.

The Jubilee Circus was in town, its colourful tents spread out in the fairground near Town Hall. You know Gorakhpur loves a good tamasha, and business had been good for the circuswalas. But one day its owner and manager, an Anglo-Indian glorying in the name of Christobel Natarajan, was found morosely sipping tea at Macedos. It was early in the day, otherwise he would have been enjoying his drink, a stiff whisky or three.

'What happens to be the matter, Master Christobel?' the waiter asked. An old man, he could address the customers with ease, even famous ones like Natarajan. After all, he was a waiter at the most iconic eatery in town.

'Our tiger is sick,' Christobel said, needing to say no more. People came to the circus for many reasons, for the clowns, for the trapeze-women in their shiny dresses, for the contortionists and the fire-eater, even for the little divas of my tribe, the pretty poms dressed in bow ties, but it was the tiger that held them all in awe with its wide yawn, its glistening red tongue as it licked its chops, its murderous grace in the arc lights, and the great big boom of its roar.

Few would see a tiger in the wild, and even those who saw the great creatures in a zoo, saw only a caged thing, robbed of its power. In the circus, with no bars between them, with that lethality prowling the circle, with sudden, terrible death just a pounce away, the audience was in a trance of such terror, it was almost ecstasy.

'I'm ruined,' Natarajan said, 'ruined. The veterinarian has looked at him, the trainer says nothing, and all the tiger does is sit in his cage, mewl and lick his hide.'

'Do you know of Baba Tota-maina?' the waiter asked. And when Christobel shook his head, the old man gestured towards the tumbledown graves across the road from the restaurant. 'He was known as the protector of the forests and all the creatures in it. They said that the parrots and mynas would speak to him, and sit upon his shoulders. For all the problems of the wild, Baba Tota-maina had the answers.'

Natarajan was a good Christian man, he had no truck with superstition, but he was also a circus owner who had tried everything else. He handed the waiter a fifty-rupee note, and told him to say a prayer for the tiger.

The next day he was back, delighted, and shoved a wad of notes into the waiter's hands. The tiger had recovered miraculously, and the circus was back in business, its star roaring its defiance to the universe.

It is said that the very next day the waiter had moved across the road and taken the job of maintaining the graves as his first occupation, and slowly the twin graves had been cleaned and converted into a glittering compound, where the poor found rest, the weary found succour, dogs were fed, and people like Knownto wandered in with their problems.

Sitting on the wall that marked the boundary of the compound now, Knownto found that he could not go in. He was far enough away from Carnegie King that the force of the man's will no longer made him bend like a reed in a strong wind, but the American was waiting at the railway station. It had been Knownto's place of power, that fabled station, and now it was something else entirely. He could not leave it, nor could he return to it with this problem unresolved.

He sat and smoked, one cigarette, then two, then three, and found his pack of Charminar empty. Crushing it in one fist, he found that the caretaker had appeared next to him, drawn to his cigarette smoke like a spirit to incense. He was very old, so old that he looked timeless. Knownto wondered briefly if he was a jinn. The caretaker said nothing, but there was a peace to his face, and Knownto, a man of secrets and silences himself, a solitary man who moved unseen in broad daylight, found himself spilling out his problem.

'Come inside,' the caretaker said, and Knownto did. The graves were covered with a green embroidered cloth and there were fresh rose petals on the cloth. Knownto followed the caretaker's example and circled the graves thrice. Then, overcome by all that had happened to him that day, he kneeled down, and as he did, he took out one crisp hundred-rupee note after another. His hand hesitated on the fifth and last, and then he laid it, too, at the edge of the graves.

The caretaker did not speak, but patted Knownto's shoulder reassuringly. Knownto had nothing to say either, he was in the hands of the Baba now.

The next days passed listlessly for Knownto, but on Wednesday he suddenly found his verve again. A casual stroll through the station and he was suddenly hundreds of rupees richer. He thought of fleeing, then. Lucknow was not so far away, and Charbagh railway station was as crowded as Gorakhpur's, it was said.

But he knew the thoughts were useless. The American would find him easily, and he was Knownto Sharma, after all, his fingers might be invisible to human eyes, but he was known to all. How far could he run?

On Thursday, his heart heavy with dread, Knownto made his way to that special set of rooms set aside for Carnegie King. There was nothing for it except to admit failure, come what may. Nothing was going to save him now.

He shooed away the dog sitting outside the door and knocked. Not waiting for an answer, he opened the door. He found the American and the caretaker from Baba Tota-maina ki kabar sitting opposite each other. A beatific smile broke out on the old man's face.

'Come on in, Knownto,' the American said, 'meet Gangu Ram.'

DOES IT CATCH MICE?

You must have heard that old joke about the Chinese dog and the Indian dog—no, not me—that meet at the border. Everyone has. How the Chinese dog, in his fancy jacket and his collar studded with rhinestones, looks down at the Indian dog and demands the respectful tribute of a bone because of how rich and powerful he is.

'You are but a stray, a fallen specimen of a once great—though not as great as ours—civilisation, merely a running dog of the capitalists,' the Chinese dog yaps. 'Look at my imperious profile, my well-fed muscles, my glossy fur. After a Century of Humiliation, we are now on top, and teaching the world to kowtow again, as it should.'

'All that may be true,' the Indian dog asks, 'but why are you on this side of the border?'

The Chinese dog looks a bit ashamed, and then says quietly, 'Well, it is nice to howl once in a while.'

It is all a lie, of course. There is no border between India and China, only the detritus of the empire that the Lamas built and lost to Gulab Singh's Dogra descendants, then to the British, and then to Mao. The only dogs that meet on the borders are Tibetan mastiffs and their counterparts from Himachal and the other hills, all full of fang and growl, with no jokes exchanged.

But the deeper lie is that of the wealth of the Chinese, because everybody knows that Deng Xiaoping, who opened that door, was not Chinese, he was from Gorakhpur, which, if you insist, would make him an Indian.

Well, everybody who knows these things knows, and everybody else would too, if they paid any attention. But this generation, yours, is a new one, fascinated by news that lasts just a minute on your mobile phones, if that long. There was a time when people would tune into the radio, to medium-wave and shortwave, when they'd listen to runaways and travelling sadhus and monks and sellers of smuggled watches from the border, and while the smoke rested lazily over the fields at sunset, they had time to think, to talk.

So it was a long time ago that Chintu figured out that Deng, the so-called Chinese leader, bore an uncanny resemblance to Prakash Mishra, whom some of them had studied with in school. In fact, Chintu had studied with him in at least three classes, although he didn't recall whether they had overlapped because he failed his fourth grade or Prakash failed his fifth.

When the newspapers began to show grainy pictures of a man who had become the Paramount Leader of China, Chintu and friends sat around and discussed the similarities between this man called Deng Xiaoping and their former schoolmate. Arun, who still carried around an old photograph from the '40s, took it out, and comparing it, they were assured that this was the same fellow, especially when they saw that familiar daft grin. It was Prakash, all right, or Pintu, as they always called him.

Pintu's story is an odd one. He wasn't even from Gorakhpur, or at least not from Gorakhpur proper. None of his group were. They were village people, and came from the smattering of houses scattered around the main town to attend the government school near the road crossing at Jungle Sub'haan Ali. That's how they knew each other. And they had a shared knowledge of the town, of their state and country and this world and the after-world, that they gathered from all the stories that would make their way around the evening fires where everybody gathered between dinner and slipping off to sleep.

Pintu's family was already rather strange. His father had worked in the house of some old zamindar in the countryside some distance from Gorakhpur city, and had assiduously been stealing land for decades while mixing increasingly large quantities of opium in his master's food, drink, and virtually everything else. It was only surprising that the zamindar didn't dance around with a dog in his arms and a poppy tucked behind his ear. By the time that the zamindar died, his sons found that Pintu's father had acquired almost as much land as they had, and what little they had was in debt. Too feeble and genteel to deal with the consequences, they retreated to the city, and Pintu's family was suddenly very rich indeed.

You would have thought that this would make for a

good and well-settled issue, but you see, all zamindars weren't like the evil lecherous stereotypes in Bollywood movies, and this one, lost in a narcotic haze, was far from an exploitative tyrant. And everybody knew that Pintu's father had managed to amass much money and a new position in society by thievery alone. Many people whispered about what had been done, and although nobody really loved the zamindars, they loved Pintu's father even less, and as I've said, the zamindar he had looted was a mild fellow and people even felt sorry for him and his brood. Pintu's family went into paroxysms defending themselves, and tried to conceal their ill-gotten wealth.

But not Pintu. As he grew from boyhood to adolescence, he was afflicted—some would say blessed—with that subtle disease called ambition. He was infected with dreams of wealth, and legitimate wealth at that. He thought of cars, and fawning drivers; he was a weird one.

It isn't as if people in the village don't dream of big things. They do. All of them will have gone to see the movies about small-town boys who make it big in the city, many of them will sing the songs to themselves and a few of them will even try out the dance moves. But dreams are dreams, ambition is something else altogether. It is an urban disease, full of constantly changing standards and violent imaginings.

While he was impatient for some city of bright lights and fast cars, for Vat 69 whisky in a bar where Helen or Bindu might come to dance and sit in his lap, Pintu did not live a life of quiet desperation in his village at the edge of our Gorakhpur, the only city he'd seen. He pretended to be a zamindar. He even tried to train a local stray to be his hunting hound, but the dog only stuck around when he had a chance to be fed, and hunted nothing more dangerous than some bones from the butcher's. What can I tell you, Pintu was mad, my grand-uncle who grew up in that village would say, recounting the story when I was a pup. But all the madness in the world can't make you become something you're not, and Pintu remained unfulfilled. All the posturing in the world can't help you pass your exams, and when Pintu continued to fail in his studies, his father finally paid off a car-shop owner in the city—there weren't too many back then—to employ his overambitious son.

This might not have been the best thing for Pintu. Every day he would have to see the rich with their wealth, while he had to be servile, to bow and scrape. But he learnt, he was a quick mimic, and despite all his madness, he was intelligent. When he came to the chowk at Jungle Subh'aan Ali in a Standard Herald, they all thought it was his. He had them completely fooled. It was only later that they learned that Pintu had just managed to steal it away for a night, having begged his father for petrol so that he could have a car to show off.

The important thing was that he didn't get caught, and his daring lie was remembered more for the daring than for the lie. Or maybe by that time people had become used to his oddities and everybody sort of knew that he'd push things too far sometime soon, and receive his comeuppance. That was what they thought—and hoped for, because every dog knows how much your species hates to see one of your own glory in good fortune, deserved or not.

Pintu was young and at the shop, in the heart of the city, every hour he saw people he wanted to copy but couldn't afford to. All the ingredients were there; all that was needed was a spark. And she came. Her name was Neetu. Neetu Singh, the daughter of one of the old families, fabulously rich in their mouldering house which even Pintu's father wouldn't have dreamed of entering. He had only stolen for a decade or two while that kind of wealth requires generations of plunder.

My grand-uncle would say, each time he told us the story: 'I saw her many years later, and although I still think that Pintu was mad to do what he did, I can understand why he did it. She was something special, that Neetu Singh, a dream from the world of movies.'

Why she encouraged mad Pintu, nobody knows. It might be just one of those cruel games that the rich play. Or it might have been because she saw something in him, some fire that was missing among the spoilt child-like half-men she knew. Even now, after so many decades, nobody knows exactly what happened, just that somehow Pintu got inside the house, and that he met her there. Maybe she had thought it would be nothing, something to laugh about. She didn't bear in mind that Pintu was ambitious, and he inevitably reached for more than he was offered.

It took only one yell from her to summon the guards. And they came swiftly, to mete out a form of justice that used wooden sticks, bamboo poles and just raw-skinned knuckles. It is a miracle that he was allowed to live, but his bones were broken, and his features rendered indescribable.

Pintu survived because his father sold much of the stolen land and paid for a doctor and hospital far beyond the means of anybody in the village. But there was nothing like plastic surgery in those days, and the best the doctor could do wasn't very good.

The nose was shortened, and became oddly rounded at the end. The whole face was shoved in, and the eyes became slits receding into his head. When his friends went to see him a month later, they couldn't recognise him. He was completely changed, and in the hospital there was this Chinese nurse, the descendant of this old Chinese family that had lived in Gorakhpur for generations, and to his friends, all racists to the core and proud of it, he almost looked like her brother. So, there was Pintu with his new face, and there was this Chinese nurse attending him, and something was growing between them, and they started to call him "Chinky baba", as cruel to him as they were to her.

They hadn't imagined that Pintu's association with the nurse would go on for much longer, but it did.

Maybe it was the violent beating that had softened his brain, or maybe it was his old disease, ambition. He knew he had failed in Gorakhpur, he would never overcome his failures here. He had to leave for somewhere, and God had delivered him into the hands of a Chinese nurse.

Within a few months of his recovery, Pintu had learned enough Chinese to get the community to open up to him. He convinced the nurse's father to employ him in their little restaurant. You can still go and eat there, I'm told. The Ming, it's called, and they make good noodles.

They are a kind lot, and never hesitate to feed strays, but don't mention Pintu. He betrayed them, you see, and even all these years later the community hasn't forgotten. After winning their trust he did more and more work with them. He proposed marriage to the nurse (and was refused) and brought business to the restaurant from all over the place, including from the villagers who were in town just for a few hours. He bullied and wheedled everybody he knew, and soon the restaurant was a booming enterprise.

In the meanwhile, he spent hours convincing the Chinese to take him along when they planned a trip back to their country. He was smart. He'd learnt Chinese by then, as I've said, and had heard them speaking about how their former homeland was surprising the world, how the initial practices of the Chinese Communists were passing and business was coming up there in a manner never seen in this part of the world. Pintu had very little idea what communism was, except that it was some kind of politics that frowned upon wealth and the good life and that, of course, was stupid. But what interested him was this: if, despite this stupid ideology, business was growing so much in that huge big country, with more people than even in India, then it was a land of opportunity. He had a chance there, and he knew it wasn't so far.

The Chinese family Pintu worked with had begun to trust him by now, or maybe they pitied him, and when three of them set off to Canton two years later, they took him with them.

But Pintu had learned from his father, and along the way the three Chinese found themselves feeling very happy and relaxed indeed, as daily doses of opium were mixed into their food. This continued all the way to China, and the very evening that they landed in Canton, Pintu made his way to the Red Guards and told them that he was very sorry to tell them that he was in the company of three opium smugglers.

He had thought that he would get some award, a way into the hierarchy of China, but he had overestimated himself once again. His travelling companions were arrested, all right, but the Red Guards didn't know what to do with Pintu. They figured he was a criminal for sure, the Cultural Revolution launched three or four years earlier was in full swing and all sorts of people were being carted off to the jail. One of the Red Guards laughed and said, 'He is our very own little Deng Xioaping!'

It was newly fashionable to blame Deng, that capitalist roader, and all of Canton was buzzing with the news that the former General Secretary of the Communist Party had been stripped of his position by the Great Helmsman, Chairman Mao, and was putting in hard labour at a tractor factory in the neighbouring province of Jiangxi. He was being spoken of as a backstabber and betrayer, somebody with a smooth tongue.

Pintu knew none of this. He had survived only

on the news that the Chinese in Gorakhpur had. But they were exiles, out of touch with the news in the country by months at the least. Pintu only knew that Deng was a powerful man, because he'd heard them say that for years, and he said to the guards in his Gorakhpuri Chinese, 'Yes, yes, I am just like Deng! Long live Deng Xiaoping!'

The Red Guards didn't know whether to laugh or not, but the Cultural Revolution rewarded only two things: brutality and cruelty. Pintu was beaten, and then beaten again, and then, out of some obscure form of viciousness, he was sent to the same tractor factory where Deng was working in Jiangxi.

People say that Deng was treated well in that factory, or at least no worse than the normal worker, but these are all lies, and everybody knows that. He was beaten and humiliated, spat upon, and made to dance for the amusement of his tormentors, to confess to crimes and apologise for them, to imagine crimes that could be apologised for. And suddenly Pintu was procured.

'This is another Deng,' the Red Guards said, and they made Pintu work beside Deng, to copy the fallen General Secretary, and mock him. In an inspired bit of cruelty, a plastic surgeon was procured, and Pintu was once again exposed to the blade. They cut him first with a red blade, and then with a blue one, and then they cut him again. The work was crude, but far better than anything that had passed before, and though you could easily tell the difference if you looked, Pintu could have passed off as Deng from a distance.

In the evenings there would be beatings, and Deng was made to recite all his famous sayings, while Pintu was made to learn them. Then both would be set up to perform, mimicking each other in a parody of parodies.

Far away, in the same country but another world, time continued its own long march. Six years after Pintu was put to work in the tractor factory Zhou Enlai, Premier of China, found himself dying of cancer, and tried to convince Mao to bring back Deng, who alone could manage a country bent towards its own destruction by the Great Helmsman. Mao hesitated, raped some more virgins and enjoyed the tortures of another dozen dissidents before finally agreeing.

But by the time the message reached the tractor factory in Jianxgi, Deng had died, the victim of old age and all the cruelties that petty minds can think up when they have a once powerful man at their mercy. Pintu, though, had survived. As had his ambition. He saw the Red Guards were terrified—for the Great Helmsman would not be denied what he wanted; death was no excuse. Pintu told the Red Guards that he would go in Deng's place and nobody would learn of the old man's death.

'But you aren't even Chinese,' the Guards protested.

'It doesn't matter if the cat is black or white as long as it catches mice,' Pintu replied, and went on to change the world.

HAGGU AND THE MAGIC BULLET

Haggu was not his real name, of course. His parents had named him Chandragupta, and he was Chandu at home, at school, and even at college, until one day that awful thing happened.

When I say he was in college, please don't be under the impression that he was studying. Few did that at DAV Degree College, Hindi medium, in Gorakhpur in the 1990s. To study they would have to have teachers. And in those years the teachers were in a long-running feud with the administration. Haggu had no idea what it was about, hardly any student did. It might have been salaries, or promotions, or a government order directing the teachers to actually report for work. All that the students knew was that half the time their classes would be cancelled, and the man who was principal one week, was not the principal next week.

I guess the students learned something. If nothing else, at least this much: the act of defiance, of organising, of mobs. These are not lessons to be sniffed at in our parts, even if they don't add up to a degree that will get you a good job.

It was not all the fault of the college, though. A college degree in those days was hardly something to make a song and dance about. Some studied, yes, and went on to universities in Allahabad, Banaras, or far off Dilli, but those students came in silently and left silently and were rarely seen again, or even remembered. For the others, for Haggu's peers, there was only Gorakhpur, and a degree did nothing for you here.

A cousin of Haggu's had finished his BA degree in double quick time, in three years. Of course, that was the scheduled time, but few were in such a rush. That cousin now worked at the petrol station in Town Hall. Haggu studiously ignored him when he went to fill up petrol in his father's Hero Honda motorcycle.

Both for his own reputation and his cousin's. What was the point of a quick degree if this is what it got you?

And then there were the glamourous dons, the Shahis, the Tiwaris, the Amarmani Tripathis of the time, with their big bungalows and big cars, armed guards and AK-47s. Now *that* was the life, of power and politics, money and women. That was what many of his peers dreamed of, rather than sitting in a shop, like the one that Haggu's father had, where he sold wiring and electrical machinery, some of it at deep discounts if you were not too particular about where it had been sourced. Haggu sat in that shop some days, but it wasn't where he wanted to be, it wasn't what he wanted to do.

He was a large boy, a man now, standing ten inches over five feet, and bulky with it; he towered over most of his classmates. He had an easy charm to him as well. It isn't surprising that he had managed to gather a small gang around him. He ate well, and his friends, or really his followers, ate well with him. If his father was bothered about money in his ledger not really matching what was in the cash drawer, he should have paid Haggu more. It was simple justice, as Haggu saw it.

You could say it was the eating that decided his fate. If you ignore all the rest, that is—the city where he was born and grew up, the college he attended, the height and bulk he acquired, the big bungalows and the big cars he saw in certain parts of the city.

They had gone to Chhote Qazipur the night before, he and his gang. They had eaten the oily qorma with the heavy dunlop rotis, and that morning he had a tight feeling in his lower gut. Not his stomach, really, but in an odd place. He had spent his time in the bathroom, smoking not one, not two, but three Capstan cigarettes, lighting one off the end of the other, and this had provided some relief, but on the way to the college to deposit his fees, it had come back, that tight feeling, and made him irritable.

There was a new boy there, in the line for the fees. Haggu knew everybody, and he did not know this boy. And the boy looked slick, with his combed hair and his jeans that did not look like the Hara ones that were available to those who made the inevitable trip north into Nepal.

But what really got Haggu's goat was the white T-shirt worn under an open shirt. It was so white, and the new kid wore it like he knew how to. Haggu had only seen one man do this, and that was the megastar Shahrukh Khan in *Darr*, or some other hit movie—he couldn't remember which—and he did not know how to feel about the man. Until recently there had been only Amitabh Bachchan as a megastar, but even Haggu had to concede that Big B looked a little too old, even—sadly—ridiculous, as a motorcycle riding, iron chain wielding Shahenshah. And Aamir Khan and Salman Khan were strictly for the girls. Shahrukh Khan, though. He was complicated—if you looked at his smooth-as-chocolate face he was a chikna, he shampooed his hair, he wept, but then he played those crazed villainous roles, he terrorized girls who did not love him back and killed the men who stood in his way. Grown, tough-talking men were crazy about him, they thronged the theatres when a Shahrukh Khan movie was playing. It was odd. And Haggu could not quite decide where his feelings lay. He did not know how to deal with the new superstar.

He decided that the new boy was easier to deal with.

'Oye, Shahrukh Chikne, don't you know how to button your shirt?' Haggu demanded of the new kid.

The boy turned around, and Haggu was startled

to realise that they were of a height, and while the boy was skinnier, he did not look like easy meat. This annoyed him further.

The boy finished looking at him, and turned back.

'I'm talking to you,' Haggu said, and put a meaty hand on the boy's shoulder, and then he was on the ground.

It took him a second to understand what had happened, that the new boy had turned quickly and punched him straight in the gut. On the uneven steps of the college in front of the grilled window behind which a hidden clerk was collecting the fees, the impact of the blow had been just enough for Haggu to lose his balance, and he had fallen heavily on the grass.

And then another thing became obvious. The punch had landed at just the right place, and with just the right force, to ease whatever knot it was that had formed in his gut, bothering him since that meal of last night. And now, as he tried to rise, Haggu was enveloped with a strong, sick odour.

He had shat himself. And in that crush of bodies in front of the college that was not something that could remain a secret. As he rose, so did the stench, and somebody hooted, '*Arre, Chandu ne to hagg diya!*'

Chandu spun around, and somebody repeated the line from behind, as he spun again, the catcalls came from his right and his left, from people safely hidden behind others as they called out the newest insult to the young man who had bullied so many of them. '*Arre Haggu! Haggu re!*'

Despite the rage that took over him, Chandu knew that there was nothing he could do right then and there, so he fled the taunts, walking all the way home as no rickshaw would let him get on, with a pack of stray dogs sniffing and howling behind him.

They got the new boy later, Haggu and his small gang, pulled him out of class, took him to the field, beat him with cricket wickets until they broke, leaving him a whimpering bloody mess that would take a month in the hospital to heal, but from then on, Chandu was Haggu, and there was nothing he could do to change the name.

Around the time that Haggu had his unfortunate baptism, a more famous encounter was taking place. It happened in that alley that runs out of Golghar, just next to the Gandhi ashram where everybody and their cousin bought kurta pyjamas. They said there were six gunmen, some said there were a dozen, but

Haggu knew this for the exaggeration it was. There had been only two, but they'd used AK 47s.

The ambush had been near-perfect. Shahi, that deranged don, was driving the white Ambassador. He was the only gangster or politician, or gangster-politician, who drove himself, with his pistol on the dashboard in front of him. The car was too large to take a U-turn in that alley, and that is where they set the ambush, one gunman on each side, in a crossfire that riddled the body of the vehicle, and the four men inside.

Three men, actually, because Shahi survived. How he managed is anybody's guess, but it might be because he was driving, paranoid, and as quick as a cat. Also, it helped that despite his overlarge reputation, he was physically quite a small man. From what they could piece together afterward, Shahi saw one of the gunmen, slammed his foot on the brakes and swung the car sharply, crouching behind the wheel as he did so. The bulk of the car's engine, and the bulk of his men, saved him from the fusillade.

More importantly, as lethal as they are, AK 47s suffer from the same problem as other submachine guns. On automatic, their magazine is empty before you realise it, and the power of automatic fire pulls the gun up and to the right. Not even the strongest man can hold one steady. You should see them at the police range, where only cops and stray dogs go. Once a year, they do their target practice. The fire of submachine guns, sten guns in the old days, AK 47s now, is always followed by a series of howls as dogs react to the sudden blurt of death that is sprayed across the field.

We dogs yowled that day too, when the shooting stopped, and the gunmen realised their second mistake. They hadn't brought extra magazines. As the shooting died down, and did not restart, Shahi popped up with his automatic and started firing back at the men sent to kill him. He emptied his magazine, nine bullets, sharp barks versus the extended howl of machine gun fire. A glancing shot took the meat off one man's shoulder. The second was clipped in the leg, he fell, got up, and continued running, not realising that his femoral artery had been nicked. He bled to death in fifteen steps.

Shahi alone emerged from it all unscathed. Or so the rumours said. More reliable sources suggested that not all his men had died, one survived. Others said that the only reason that Shahi had not run after the second gunman and killed him with his bare fists and empty gun, was because he was limping from a wound. And everybody knew that the only person who would know about the injury was Dr Ralla at the government medical college.

That was a strange relationship. She was a surgeon with no patients until Shahi turned up. What can I say, Gorakhpur used to be progressive. We had such a literary scene that Premchand applied to get a job here as a schoolteacher, a job he left after hearing Gandhi's speech in 1921. And we had Raghupati Sahai, that flaming queen who called himself Firaq Gorakhpuri—I would have traded my freedom to become his pet just to listen to his poetry, for his blasphemy, for his style, but that sly hound had already died before I was pupped. And not only men of letters—do you know we had Shibhan Lal Saxena of the Kisan Mazdoor Union, the Gorakhpuri representative on the Constituent Assembly, a man so committed to democracy he survived being shot against Nepal's royalist forces in a demonstration there?

We have fallen far from those days, and nothing illustrated that so much as the lack of patients at

Dr Ralla's door. She was a surgeon, and in these parts people would trek a hundred miles to come to Gorakhpur because it had the only decent government hospital. But it seemed that people were willing to die rather than let somebody of what your vile lot call low caste, a beneficiary of reservation, touch their flesh to heal them.

From beyond the grave, Ambedkar had helped Dr Ralla get her seat in the medical examinations, but it was her will, her determination, that had borne her through the scorn of her teachers, the spittle and taunts of her classmates, to finally get her degree. And of that she'd had enough. Why else would she have chosen surgery, the discipline that reached deeper than skin, that ventured into the flesh, blood and bones? The so-called upper castes had once not even allowed the shadow of her people to fall upon them, so she chose something that would allow her to cut in so deep that the supposed pollution of her touch could never be expunged. Oh, she was a fierce one, but all the fierceness in the world will not get you patients if they will not come.

Then Shahi had appeared. Not as a patient himself, that would have to wait until after the ambush, when he'd lie on his belly, his hairy buttocks exposed to the cold probing metal of her scalpel and pincers. No, the first time he came was with one of his men who'd fractured his arm badly.

She had made no comment, asked no questions, although she was no fool, and knew of his criminality. But then what did she care, trapped in a system that treated her as worse than a criminal? She did her job, and she did it well, and Shahi's men came to her for treatment every few weeks after that, even for things that were not a surgeon's job. And slowly, ever so slowly, others made their way. Even some Dalits, who had so far feared that if they went to a doctor, one of their own, whom nobody else visited, their welcome back to their villages would send them back to the hospital again, broken or burnt. But Shahi's name was a shield around her, and by extension, them. A weapon against the weaponised world they lived in.

It was odd that it was Shahi in his white Ambassador car who had arrived at Dr Ralla's door, and not Paswan, the don of the oppressed castes, in his bullet-proof Matador van—after all, it went against the grain of the Thakur clan that Shahi lorded over. But the games of dons and politicians are subtle ones. Wasn't one of the original dons supposedly patronised by Sanjay Gandhi, a wannabe don in his own right? But he's respectable now, that don, and I don't think anybody has the courage to ask him that question in the grand kothi that he usurped from that businessman, the kothi with high walls that sits in the middle of town.

Ah, I digress, one story runs into another, but this is Gorakhpur, and our history is like our soil, all mixed up in the past and present, nothing quite pure, legend, hearsay and tall tales all running into each other. You need the nose of a dog to tell you fact from lie, and even then you can never be sure.

That day, after Dr Ralla had extracted the lumpy copper-coloured little cylinder from Shahi's left buttock and dropped it into the steel surgical tray before stitching the wound up, all she said was, 'You're lucky. It must have been a ricochet.'

Shahi only laughed. He was still laughing when the bandage was done, and he jumped off the bench, grabbed the bloody nub of lead and washed it himself. 'I will have this set in gold,' he declared. 'I will wear it over my heart.'

And that is what he did, although legend says that

the goldsmith applied some odd procedure, and when the light of the sun caught the bullet, hanging on a gold chain just above the opened second button of Shahi's shirt, it would glint blue, but in the light of the moon it would glint red, like blood.

That bullet, that ambush, was the making of Shahi's legend. The use of AK 47s against him, weapons that people had only seen on movie screens, and that too in the heart of the city, testified to his power—somebody very powerful wanted him dead, and that somebody had failed. Who that was, nobody ever really found out, although there were a spate of killings that followed. Whether it was revenge, or merely the scent of opportunity, is also not known, but soon there was nobody who would directly challenge Shahi. The other dons did not disappear, but they made way.

Haggu's career followed a similar trajectory. The fight that named him, and the beating in defence of his honour that followed, cemented his reputation. He became the man to be feared in Baxipur, then Reti, and then all the way to Urdu Bazar. The problem was the name. It still brought up a snigger—when he was not looking. Once, a smart person had the idea of merely wrinkling his nostrils, not saying anything, but Haggu was not one who took even such a minor slight in his stride. The beating that followed this time had a salutary effect, and soon men with even a winter cold would find a way not to be around Haggu, in case the sniffling was misperceived. He was even known to kick dogs who sniffed around him, and we quickly learned to stay well away from the fellow.

Haggu burned to prove himself, and maybe the derogatory nickname made him burn all the hotter. He would take risks that no normal person would. It is said that it was Haggu who convinced Chintu Saxena to rent out the guns from his shop.

Dacoities and burglaries were a fact of life in and around Gorakhpur then, as they are now, which isn't unusual in this country. The police managed to solve most cases, or at least those that they wanted or needed to solve, because they knew that while dacoits are hard to trace—the people, that is—the equipment they use marks them out and can be traced: the motorcycles, the jeeps or cars, the weapons. But around the time that Haggu's reputation began to really grow, there was a spate of dacoities in this area that left the police baffled. These robberies were complicated; the men did not use kattas, the ubiquitous countrymade revolvers, whose gunsmiths the police could track down, if they so wanted. No, these dacoits were using fine weapons, 12-bore shotguns, rifles, even a pistol or two.

As the robberies intensified and continued for months, the pressure on the police was acute. It was only by chance that a young Deputy Superintendent of Police, on her first posting as an active officer and given the usual grunt work of checking paperwork, noticed a problem with the inventory at Chintu Saxena's gun-shop. Normally this would have involved nothing more than money changing hands, but she was unusually honest, a Tamil out of place in Gorakhpur. Worse, she had a keen eye for detail. When Chintu failed at his clumsy attempt at bribery, he made things worse. And then, in haste to smoothen things out, he had the missing weapons produced.

But Chintu made a stupid error, one that his father, who'd died of a heart attack some years ago, might have taught him, had the boy not preferred spending all his waking hours drinking and whoring with his friends. Chintu forgot to clean the guns, and the guns had been fired.

The two shotguns and the pistol had been used in

a robbery only a week before, and the .25 pistol slug had been recovered from the wooden frame of the doorway where one of the overenthusiastic robbers had fired in order to cajole the staff and lone customer at the jewellery store to hurry up.

The DSP put two and two together, and Chintu Saxena found himself in jail.

It was Haggu, we know, who started Chintu on this road. Gun sales were plummeting, with T.N. Seshan cracking down on the racket of booth capturing—remember him, the terrifying new Election Commissioner of the time? But Haggu convinced Chintu that there was a new market in loaning weapons. And it was Haggu who had the contacts with local boys in need of untraceable weapons; he who then fenced the stolen goods.

Chintu sang like a canary, the police needed to do very little—all the drinking and whoring and smoking up in the shop his father left him had made Chintu Saxena soft as a Jaipuri razai. But Haggu had been careful. There were too few threads that tied him to anything directly. He had not shared all his information with Chintu or even his gang, certainly not any about where he had fenced the goods. In a city like Gorakhpur, where goldsmiths and jewellers abounded, it was impossible to track down what had been stolen. And unlike Chintu, Haggu had known whom to bribe.

He was under watch, but the DSP was transferred within a few months, and things went on as they were before, except that Haggu was now known as Haggu Badmash, and even the dons took an interest in his doings. They wrinkled their noses while doing it, of course, as did their big men, and this Haggu had to bear.

Fame accompanied by that name was just more salt in the wound. It may have been what pushed him to the next level. Of learning how to use the supplies at his own father's shop more creatively—the wires and switches and other electrical hardware. He was smart, and experimented far from the city, on the highway to Nepal, where there is a lot of forest and few people, maybe a group of banjaras now and then. It was where he perfected his craft.

It is said that Haggu designed the bomb that was rolled under Paswan's bulletproof van, proving, yet again, that armour may save you from a bullet, but will render you to paste if a bomb explodes beneath you. Nobody took Haggu's name, although the group of boys who did the deed, for whom he made the bomb, were from his DAV days.

It was then that Shahi called him to his house, poured him a drink, and said, 'Haggu Bumwaala, you are now one of us,' and laughed. And with that the name 'Haggu Bum' became part of the folklore of the city, an improvised but lethal bomb that could take down a don, a bomb that could breach a bulletproof van. It was the ultimate weapon, with a name to be laughed at.

Haggu had burned so long at the name he had failed to get rid of, no matter what he did. Now he burned even more that after all his efforts, and after his greatest success, all he had done was add his bum, the bum that had betrayed him, to his hated nickname.

And he burned in envy of Shahi, the don who had a magic that nobody could touch him; the don who had beaten death. And he burned because Paswan had been part of Shahi's group. Haggu's role in Paswan's murder made him easy prey for Shahi. The don could have snuffed out Haggu's life with a snap of his fingers and most would have called it justice, but Shahi was a crazy man, he blamed the rising power instead, the power sitting in the Temple, where people increasingly went to have their disputes managed, and said he would break down the doors of the Temple if the murderers of Paswan were not brought to book. And Haggu he kept close.

Paswan's murder was part of the closing of the loop. The state government had formed a special task force to crack down on the dons of the railway contracts. Of course, things were not so simple as that. Politics and policing rarely are.

You see, after the Biharis betrayed us, people like Paswan, Shahi and all the dons were marked men.

Let me explain. The Biharis betrayed us, although they don't hate us and we don't hate them. We are both Purabia, after all, speak the same language, the Doordarshan Bhojpuri channel is broadcast from Gorakhpur, after all. We are family. But this was money, and as everybody knows there is no biradari when it comes to wealth, or if there is, it a biradari of betrayal.

They took the railway ministry in Dilli, the Biharis, and they kept it. And you know how much the railway means to our Gorakhpur, headquarters of the North Eastern Railway. With the ministry went the new trains, and with that the contracts for food, for blankets, for all sorts of things that trains needed and the dons of Gorakhpur had provided, at a price. Even Haji Mastan, that big Bombay don, had his people working in Bahraich.

With the contracts gone, the dons became increasingly superfluous. In fact, they became a nuisance; reminders of a time that was best forgotten, especially as the light shone on their activities reflected off the Temple as well.

A special task force was set up, there were raids, and encounters—those strange episodes of handcuffed prisoners suddenly managing to grab a weapon, and always, always, ending up killed in the supposed firefight that followed. Villagers said they saw the men being shot down by the side of the road, but who believes the words of villagers, they are easy to ignore, like the howling of stray dogs.

Somehow, though, Shahi had escaped—not only escaped, but had prospered. He still drove like a madman with his pistol on the dashboard, and nothing, it seemed, could touch him. And around his neck, never removed, was a gold chain on which hung a bullet that they said glinted one colour in the day, and another in the night.

Haggu wanted that bullet. He wanted it bad. He was sick with the wanting of it, wretched, but he was now also Shahi's man, his liaison, his bombmaker, and sometimes, his pimp.

They say it was a woman, a woman Haggu procured, who was Shahi's downfall. And another woman, an upright Tamil cop, the Deputy Inspector General of the police, who helped Haggu set it up. She had been transferred out of Gorakhpur for her competence once, but it was the same competence that now meant she oversaw a wider fiefdom of which Gorakhpur was a small part. And she knew them all, had forgotten nothing, not even how slippery Haggu was, and now she used that slipperiness for her own ends. What he was promised, we do not know, but Shahi was killed in Lucknow. It was Dr Ralla who did the autopsy, though, in Gorakhpur. She noticed that the thin gold necklace Shahi always wore was missing, but she never mentioned that in her report.

And Haggu? Well, Haggu disappeared. There is no record of anybody by that name, no official file with even the suggestion of that name survives, although they say there was a fire the day before Shahi was killed, in the old police headquarters. A lot of papers burned, with names that no longer needed to be remembered.

On the highway to Lucknow, though, there is a large ostentatious hotel called Chandragupta Inn. They have a very tough policy on health, they say, and if any guests even have the beginnings of a cold, just a sniffle, they are shown the door.

THE GOLDEN RENDEZVOUS

He had a disease, Tharki did, what is called White-itis, or white-skin disease, although it sounds rougher and more evocative in our tongue: *gori chamdi ki bimari.* Truth be told, Tharki was not alone in this regard. You could say the whole town, the whole country, all of Akhand Bharat, that undivided India of the imagination that flows all the way to Siberia, suffers from it.

Your kind, you fawn so embarrassingly over those firangis with pale skin, make yourselves smaller than you are, as if it were some weird affliction where *they* have the symptoms but *you* suffer. Even Tilak, that great freedom fighter—you know, the one who died under lathis, with his skull broken—even he suffered from it. What else would explain his wild hypothesis that the people of India were descended from some White race born of the North Pole? As if the journey outward from Africa, the tens of thousands of miles, the savannah, the terror of the wild in which humans had just about the same muscle mass as a house cat—a small house cat, at that—was not glorious and awesome enough.

In Gorakhpur we have our own set of kala Angrez. Like Mehdi sahib, recently departed. It was said of him that he would step out with an umbrella when the BBC predicted rain in London.

But Tharki's case was a little different. He had another agenda over this normal abnormality that your kind suffer from. His nickname, more real than the one his parents gave him, reveals that clearly enough. It was not even a play on his family name, he was no Thakur or Thakkar, nor did this have anything to do with caste, although everything does. I have heard people argue that this affliction of your kind, this White-itis, is also a form of caste, for the privileged could hide from the sun, could shelter under umbrellas held over their heads by the oppressed, and naturally their pampered, pale pallor became the colour divine, all else inferior and impure. Why, even your blue-skinned gods must be made pale in their latest incarnations on television, or so I am told. We dogs suffer from all sorts of diseases, but colourism isn't one of them. We are colour blind, you are not, and which of us has gained, and which of us has lost—well, you make up your mind about that.

But as I was saying, Tharki's disease was the usual White-itis, but also something else, something more straightforward. Simpler. He just wanted to have sex, but with a white woman. A disease compounded, you could say.

The thought entered his head without warning, like some airborne parasite that takes over body, mind and soul—I know because I was there when Tharki was touched by the hand of fate, or that of a white woman, and we all know that is one and the same thing.

They were at the train station that day, as they often were, the boys, analysing. It is something that Gorakhpuris are very good at. Warsi, one of Tharki's seniors at the Railway School, had explained it succinctly. 'India is a nation of analysts. One man will do the job, and a hundred will stand around him, analysing.'

And so they called themselves 'The Analysts', the three of them, Guddu, Kabir and Tharki. 'Let's analyse Gol Ghar,' Kabir would say, and they would be off.

It was not that they were bad students, in fact the problem was the opposite. All three of them were good at their studies, even in the Railway School, which was one of the best in the city. But this brought its own problems. They had too much time on hand, and demands—such as sitting in for somebody else for an exam. Sometimes they could refuse, but not when it came to their seniors. At thirteen, fourteen, a year or two made a big difference in bulk and height, and when one of the older kids loomed over them, the horizon of their choices narrowed considerably.

So, they analysed in their free time, and often enough found themselves at the railway station, for there was so much happening there, at all hours, except perhaps between midnight and six in the morning, when boys from proper families could not be seen outside their homes. The sea of people at the station always offered something new. You never knew when a train was going to be delayed, or for how long, and the automated voice of the woman announcing how deeply saddened she was that the train was going to be delayed by an hour, two hours, half a day, or cancelled altogether, led to a multitude of reactions amongst the people gathered on the platform.

Also, they were Railway boys. Technically they should have bought platform tickets, or been subject to a fine for loitering there, but their jackets—with the school emblem proudly displayed—offered them some sort of protection. It was a perk, and in a country where government salaries are rarely substantial, people learn early to make use of any perk that comes their way.

Tharki, in particular, analysed the Wheeler & Co shop. It stocked all the popular magazines and books, and while he glanced at the former, his real interest was in the latter. With the small money gathered at festivals—one rupee here, another there, a whole tenner by a generous aunt—he could, once in a while, afford a book. It was 20 rupees for a Louis L'Amour paperback and 30 for an Alistair MacLean. He had even managed to buy an Erle Stanley Gardner, *The Case of the Perjured Parrot*, but it was nowhere as interesting as the cover had led him to believe.

You would have thought he might have taken furtive, frequent glances at the row of James Hadley Chase novels with their racy covers, or those of Jonathan Black, one of them with a nude woman sprawled across the cover, but he was not there yet. Anyway, they were too pricey for his pocket. Also, his mother would beat him with a stick if she found them in his bag.

Malik ji, who managed the Wheeler & Co store, had developed a fondness for Tharki. It did not mean much, because Malkiji also had a stick that he was more than happy to use on somebody filching a book, or flipping through a magazine without buying it, but he would allow Tharki to read a page or two of a book because he knew the lad would somehow find the money to buy it, sooner or later, once his interest was kindled.

That day Tharki was a page or so into MacLean's *The Golden Rendezvous*, wondering what a Balenciaga was. And wondering how you pronounced 'rendezvous'. He could not figure it out. No one in school, not even their English teacher, had ever actually spoken the word. It seemed to him this was one of those special words that separated the truly educated and stylish from the pretenders. There was, in other words, more to it than met the eye. Maybe the 's' at the end also had a 'z' sound? He tried it, speaking it under his breath, but it felt incomplete, that 'vouz', it had no sophistication. He tried it again, then again, and he heard himself say 'rendezvouzous'. He whispered it to himself thrice, and each time it grew in significance and sophistication. Yes, this was it.

Tharki was a reader, but not really a speaker of the language. A word like this sounded glamourous, and so he stretched it, adding a vowel and a consonant—he prided himself on his grammar—that his eyes told him were not there. And yet it made sense to his mind. This is how you humans are. Your senses will tell you something straight and true, but your minds will still twist it into a jalebi. And yet, maybe that is your glory too, because jalebis are absolutely delicious—especially after a samosa!

It was at this moment that the hand of Fate rose up and slapped him a tight one.

'Oye, what's that?' Guddu said.

'Hain?' asked Kabir, scanning right while Guddu was looking at something left of them, a scrum building up in the distance.

'That way,' Guddu said, "can you see the firangi?"

'Oh,' Kabir replied, master of great phrases and rejoinders.

Guddu grabbed Tharki's arm and said, 'Leave the book, you don't have any money anyway. Let's check that out.'

Reluctantly, Tharki put the book back on the rack, very obviously indicating to Malik ji that he had not folded the pages or marked the spine in anyway. As one, The Analysts marched down the station to figure out what the fuss was about.

It was their job.

As they drew closer, they realised that a group of men were clustered around a foreign woman, blonde ponytail sticking out behind her head, who stood half a foot taller than the poor, befuddled ticket examiner, whom she was badgering with queries. There was even the obligatory stray dog showing an interest, and that was me, young but already curious about anything involving a bit too much, or too many.

The crowd parted for The Analysts. No, that is not the correct description. Amoeba-like it opened and gathered them in, pushing them through until the three young boys—they would have called themselves men, Guddu even had something of a down on his upper lip that he insisted was a moustache—were right up in the thick of action.

At the sight of their uniforms, the ticket examiner was overcome with relief. 'Can you please tell her,' he said in Hindi, 'that I have no idea when the train will come beyond what is written at the information board?'

'Hain?' said Kabir. Guddu said nothing. So it was Tharki who did a quick translation.

The tall woman turned to him, and Tharki was pinned in place by her penetrating blue eyes. 'But the board keeps changing,' she said in a Nordic accent that would have made her English all that much more alien to the ticket examiner. 'Five times. Five times it has said one hour more. Now again it says one hour more.'

Tharki flushed, not so much at her gaze, but because all the dozens of people surrounding her were now looking at him. He felt the honour of Hindustan rested upon his shoulders, it made him nervous. But he was a Railway School boy. He rose to the challenge.

'Sir,' he asked the ticket examiner, 'do you know where it has reached? Has it crossed Gonda?'

The little man said, 'It left Gonda station fifteen minutes ago.'

With a quick calculation, Tharki told the foreign woman, 'You have at least two hours.'

The relief on the woman's face brought on by his confident response gladdened Tharki's heart. He had defended the honour of his homeland. He felt like Porus telling Alexander that even a defeated king should be treated like royalty.

'Oh, that is very helpful. Two hours. I can go and get something to eat. Is there somewhere you would recommend?'

This was a new thing. Now Tharki was more than a translator. He was his own man being asked about advice.

'Kwality, in Gol Ghar, is very good.' It was beyond his budget, and even his parents had never gone there, so it must be good, he reasoned. Feeling supremely in control, he decided to use the new word he had learned. 'If you take a rickshaw from outside and come straight back, you will have time to make it for your rendezvouzous.'

Her brow furrowed, and he figured that the word was new to her as well. 'In time to catch the train,' he explained helpfully.

'Oh,' she said, and stuck out her hand, 'thank you very much.'

Very gingerly, watched by his fellow Analysts, and the dozens of other analysts, Tharki shook her hand. There was whistling, hooting, clapping, and general exultation from the crowd. Tharki was the hero of the hour, defender of the nation, equal to—nay, superior to—the firangis. He had held a white woman's hand.

He blushed. It would normally not have been obvious with his dusky skin. But in this case his face had turned the colour of a ripe eggplant. The tourist dropped her hand somewhat in alarm, but the damage had been done.

The boy was in love. Worse, he was in lust. Things were happening to him that he did not understand, especially in parts of his body below his belt. He just stood there with his hand outstretched as the puzzled foreigner left, and the crowd slowly dispersed.

'Oye,' said Guddu. 'What do we do now?'

The question brought Tharki back to earth from wild fantasies of kisses, full on the lips, and blue eyes. It also brought home to him the embarrassment of trousers strained by a rather painfully engorged part of his body.

Very casually he put his hands in the pockets of his school jacket and pushed them ahead, hiding the indignity. 'I have to get back home.'

And when the others raised their eyebrows in surprise, he shrugged, his hands still in his pockets, 'Mother said.'

The eyebrows descended. All of them knew that mothers set unreasonable demands, but these demands had to be met.

'See you tomorrow,' said Kabir, finally getting a full sentence together, and pleased with himself for getting it out whole.

'Tomorrow,' agreed Guddu, and The Analysts disbanded, with Tharki walking much slower than the others, his stride somewhat crablike, a scuttle.

He had mentioned his mother, but the parent he should have named was his father, because the real truth is that Tharki should actually have been called Tharki Junior. His father was famously the greatest lecher that the State Bank of India in Gorakhpur had seen, either in the City Branch or in the one on Bank Road. If a woman was withdrawing money when he was the teller, the process would take at least five times as long as it otherwise did. This was far above the average lechery, which slowed down the line for only twice as long. It was so bad that he'd been finally shifted to a post where he had no interaction with customers.

Not that there were any complaints, rather the opposite. But that was the problem. He was a successful lecher. This was unexpected. To be a lecher was not such a big deal. As Tharki's mother would often say, half in lament, half in contempt, 'All men are like that.' But to succeed as a lecher, to charm not one, but many, *that* was an achievement, and a perplexity.

None of this was known by Tharki, of course, he was too young. Although the years of growth were upon him, he had not yet reached the heights at which these conversations were conducted. He did not know that what he had come into was part of his inheritance, a curse or a treasure—and all treasures are curses of one sort or another—but definitely his own.

The next few days were hard for him. He had hit puberty a while ago, but now it hit back, and hit back hard, in disturbed, fevered dreams of blue eyes and the memory of a firm grip on his hand. At first, he vowed not to wash his hand. But his mother would rather he starved than touch food in her house without first washing his hands—she had a very low opinion of men in matters of personal hygiene. Who knew what all they did with their hands? She didn't even trust them to remember that the right hand, the eating hand, was never to be used to wash their bum.

Why humankind needs to wash or wipe its arse at all is a mystery not only to my species but to every other on this planet. It must be a deep flaw in your evolution, but let us not digress.

Tharki washed his hand, and ate, but the fever did not die down. He started spending so much time in the bathroom that his mother felt he was ill, and the drawn expression on his face did not help.

Then, another, more intimate, tragedy hit him. He discovered his father's collection of newspaper-bound books one afternoon when he was alone in the house. The small cupboard with glass panels, which also contained a bottle of Bagpiper Whisky and three trophies won at inter-college badminton tournaments, was always locked, and Tharki sometimes tugged at the doors when his parents were out, curious about the books. That afternoon the doors swung open. The books were all the same size, the same thickness, like issues of *Reader's Digest.* He pulled one out and flipped it open. And he was drowned in tales of such pornographic detail that his brain shut down as all the blood in his body rushed to a single place.

It was *The Human Digest: The Journal of Sexual Behaviour*—they all were, different volumes and numbers. And all of the stories, each of which sucked all breath out of him and made his head spin, were set in America, a land of such violently sexual debauchery that he would later wonder how anybody got anything done, what with the nurses, the yoga instructors, the tennis coaches, the schoolteachers, even the nuns, oh my God, having sex, indoors and out, in ways he hadn't thought possible.

He knew then, more clearly than he had known anything in his life of thirteen years, that America was where he had to go. It was the place where he would finally find his golden rendevoozus.

The worst thing was, as Tharki drowned in a sea of hormones, he had no one to call out to, nobody who could rescue him, throw him a lifeline, tell him that this would pass, that it was, as Shakespeare wrote, only a rose by another name, whose thorns had made young men bleed through the ages. This was Gorakhpur, there was nothing like sex education. In fact, sex and education were two trains that ran in opposite directions, super-fast expresses. The closest one got to sex education was in the sly tales told by older students, and in terms of either sex or education, they left a lot out.

Tharki suffered alone, and his affliction grew in him, both for what he wanted, and where he thought his desire might finally be consummated.

Of course, he could not completely hide what was happening. The trick with the jacket, the crablike walk, the excuse about his mother's tasks, they could be used once, twice, and maybe thrice at the most, in some variety or combination, but after that the jig was up.

In actual fact, his cover was blown when he snuck one of those damned *Human Digests* into school in his bag.

It was not unusual for Tharki to be reading a book, but the intensity of his absorption in this one was extreme, so much so that he did not hear the senior who addressed him in the playground, or addressed him again, or even when he walked over. Only when the senior snatched the book from his hand, saying,

'Let's see what the runt has got,' that Tharki realised, dimly, what was happening.

'Hey, give me that,' he said. But the senior held him off with one hand, and started reading aloud. It was a story involving a grocer, a rather underclad customer, and vegetables—lots of vegetables. Even the senior choked, turning shades of colour that should not have been humanly possible. But then, even the three years between him and Tharki did not mark much of a journey on the path to maturity. Frankly, among most men of your kind the path is rarely ever embarked upon, and soon abandoned.

This may explain why Tharki's christening happened so quickly and so completely that even one of the teachers mistakenly called out the name during the morning roll call and Tharki answered.

This was the second tragedy, the deeper one, for it foreclosed any opportunity for normal interaction that Tharki might ever have had with girls. It was not as if talking to girls was a common occurrence, but it did happen, and Tharki was an unusually personable, even charming, young lad. Except that now he bore this frightening nickname like a brand, like the mark of Cain upon his brow that told others of his crime, and to beware.

Is it any surprise, then, that he was left with only his dreams of fulfilment, of a desire that could only be quenched in some land far away, an America of the imaginings, full of blue eyes and red Balenciagas, whatever they were?

He even lost his standing among The Analysts, who did not want to be thought of as tharkis, too. No one would take them seriously, everyone would snigger, and what if their mothers found out?

Tharki was left with nothing except his studies. He did well, exceptionally well. Whereas the rest of the students, the best of the best, fought for a position in the examination for the bank jobs, the railway jobs, and the thousand other government jobs that are advertised on posters plastered across the city, Tharki made it to the shortlist of one of the country's best engineering colleges.

There, at least, one would think, he would find himself among his own. With their days filled with studies, and maybe one girl in a class of 60 students, the engineering college boys are known for their mad pranks, and the stink of their overactive hormones. But Tharki's name followed him even there, and it was the name that tripped him up, bound him, gave him a stoop because it was simpler to look at his feet than at people's faces. His crime might actually have made him a star among the boys here, but his name made him ridiculous, even the well-meaning could not help but snigger. And Tharki knew that only across the black water, across the cursed seas, would he ever find release.

But engineering college was also the making of Tharki. Most people have forgotten those days, but that was when the internet first entered your lives, with those slow-speed modems clittering and clacking as they struggled to download the world on to your computers. Everyone watched with bated breath as the red lights stuttered and then went blue, opening the door to the information superhighway.

In reality, though, it was more like a dirt track those days, with massive gates and fortifications. You remember VSNL, Videsh Sanchar Nigam Limited, the department set up not to enable but practically disable international communication? The VSNL servers only led you to a log in page, and you needed the access codes for your little bucket of bits and bytes. And beyond that were paywalls that demanded credit card information, and much else.

What was a formidable barrier to the best of them, even the teachers hacking away late at night, was merely a challenge for lonely, studious Tharki, forced to hide in his room. He was a driven man who wanted to escape the subcontinent of Silk Smitha to the far uplands of Ursula Undress, and he was an Analyst, after all.

The codes crumbled under his onslaught, and soon he had a diary of log-ins that were the supposed secrets safe in the bowels of VSNL. The credit card information was too difficult, and too criminal, for him to attempt, so he broke the protocols, examining the codes that Netscape allowed him to see off the pages, and subverting it ever so slightly.

It was not easy. Porn was the gold of the new century, powering the traffic of a hundred million horny people across the globe, the fuel that drove the internet boom of a billion unfulfilled desires. Beyond the appetisers, though, the feast was well guarded. All that the websites of pornographic content would offer was a peek, and then the dragon—the demand of credit card information—would appear. But Tharki found a way, a wily Hobbit uncovering the hidden weakness in the armour.

On the day that the centrefold of Miss March in all her pulchritude unfolded pixel by pixel from *Hustler* on his screen, Tharki let out a small sigh of relief. You would think it would be a yowl of triumph after all that he had been through, but no, this was a soft sound, a laying off of a burden, Atlas soothing his tired muscles after setting down the world.

This was the second year of his degree, and the achievement marked him as a prodigy, one whose powers were unmatched. Soon, even his seniors were lining up at his door, to beg the favour of a code, or the more ambitious, of how to rejig code itself. He was generous with the former, miserly with the latter. There could be but one Analyst, and it was he.

By the end of the third year, his fame had seeped beyond the college boundaries, and at the college festivals where nerdy guitar freaks struggled to sing yet another terrible rendition of 'Hotel California', Tharki was mobbed by admirers. One professor from IIT Delhi even tried to poach him for his programme for the final year.

When the first job offer came, just as he began his final year, nobody was surprised, and then he was deluged. But Tharki, who had waited for so long, waited just a little while longer, until that one offer came winding his way from California, the coveted H1B visa almost guaranteed. His time had come, and America was finally beckoning to him to keep his promise of the that golden rendezvous—by now, he had learned to pronounce it as the high priests of language do, but the nature of it, what it was to him, had not changed.

He accepted. Of course he accepted. They say he had an office in Malibu, the windows overlooking the beach, where female bodyguards exactly like those in that show, *Baywatch*—which nobody in Gorakhpur admitted to watching but with whose plotlines and necklines they were all intimately familiar—cavorted for his delight. They say he cracked the Y2K problem like a pistachio in his fingers, and ate the goodness inside. You have seen him in those pictures, that man with wavy hair, that grin, standing next to a Saudi prince and the Russian programmer; you see him next to Prince Andrew and Jeffrey Epstein.

Some people wonder what happened, if his story finally achieved its happy ending, if he did end up with a blonde on his arm, her blue eyes contrasting with the red of her Balenciaga dress. But that is the wrong question. It misunderstands who Tharki was, what his tharak, his restless lust, his desire, was.

It wasn't about sex, really. Lust made him, but it wasn't about sex.

Tharki was Tharki because of a desire that unhoused him, unroofed him, threw him out on a road to an impossible destination, made him a stranger to his own. His tharak was what drove him to part the borders of land and sea; it was his Ithaka, it was what set him free. It was in itself always his golden rendezvous.

AUTHOR'S NOTE

When Ravi first suggested I write about Gorakhpur, I wasn't sure I wanted to. To be honest, I only said yes because I hoped he would forget about it. Not that there was any lack of stories about my hometown, just that most of them are embarrassing in the extreme.

It isn't just the content, but also the way we speak in our little cities and towns, how we draw the panorama of the world in such a way as if we are always smackdab in the centre of it all. In our telling, all of history, mythology, and every single monumental happening in the world is inevitably about us.

And yet, and yet, listening to my uncle, Habib

Ahmad, tell the tale of my great-great-grandfather being sentenced to hang after the 1857 Uprising, or to Abba telling me tales of tiger hunts, or reading Shahid Amin on Chauri Chaura or Alok Rai on Gandhi's trip to Gorakhpur—is that wrong? Is it delusional, self-important? If were to tell the story of India, what would be more important—some exquisite museum exhibit in Delhi, or the huge old *naashtedaan* in which food was transported to Gorakhpur jail to feed my grandfather's brother and his collegemate Mahant Digvijaynath, the then Mian Sahib, and a host of others?

Of course, not all the stories in this collection are true, or even partially true, in the strictest sense of the term. They are fiction, and I have borrowed from here or there. Usmaan told me of a lawyer in Srinagar who had a habit of throwing street dogs at people, Basharat and Satya cooked up the character of Tharki with me during a memorable bullshit session at Ganga Dhaba—Satya insists he saw Tharki at the New Jalpaiguri railway station. And while I did get into a quarrel or two in DAV Degree College, it was not with Haggu Bumwaala.

That said, I have tried to preserve something of

the taste of my father's city in these tales, and I have written partially to hear him laugh and correct me, to elaborate on why Macedos was such an institution, or why the railway mafia worked the way it did. A writer is made by his or her readers, or at least I am. If the tales wind and wander in their particular way, it is because I am talking to them: To Sabah, of course. To Apa, Ateeq bhaijaan and Atika, who have gone so far away. To Nilima di, Philipp, Ka, Jha, Hartosh, Mandavi, Vatsala, Neha, Kaicker, Penny, and all those I hold in my mind's eye when I try to tell a story.

And in talking to them, in trying to wrap myself around half a world in an effort to make these stories make sense, I find I have done exactly what I complained about: I've made the world revolve around Gorakhpur.

It is my mitti, I guess it will have its way.